Second Thoughts

Second Thoughts

Ideas Recycled

Ray Owen

Sketches by
Luanne Schwegal
Jack Jordan

John Wesley Press / San Antonio, Texas

SECOND THOUGHTS
IDEAS RECYCLED

Library of Congress Control Number 00-132160
ISBN 0-9662905-1-8

Printed in the
United States of America
First Printing: May 2000

John Wesley Press
The United Methodist Church
Southwest Texas Conference
P.O. Box 781149
San Antonio, Texas 78278-1149

MANUFACTURED IN THE UNITED STATES OF AMERICA

Gift of appreciation

In early childhood, I was taught that it was more blessed to give than to receive. For a few years that concept seemed strange if not questionable. The longer I have lived, however, the more convinced I have become that the joy of giving far exceeds the benefits of receiving.

I dedicate this book to the delegates who represent the marvelous clergy and lay members of the Southwest Texas and Rio Grande conferences of The United Methodist Church. I offer this gift as my inadequate attempt to say "thank you" for all the assets you have deposited so abundantly into my life.

The words on these following pages flowed from my pen to be published in weekly newspaper columns. My fondest hope is that each of these "Second Thoughts" might find its way to bless your life—perhaps for a second time. Should the pages of this book succeed in accomplishing that, then I shall have certification once again that it is indeed more blessed to give than to receive.

Ray Owen
San Antonio, Texas
Spring 2000

Contents

Foreword

Ideas are like cosmic dust. They come flitting at us from all directions with comet speed. In milliseconds they flash through our minds before zipping off into random oblivion.

Every once in a while, an idea is worthy of being grabbed and pulled back for further evaluation and application. That's what this book is all about. It's about fleeting thoughts recaptured for further study so that their intrinsic value might be aptly appreciated and applied to life.

Many of these "second thoughts" were triggered by some incident that erupted in the course of daily routine. Others were triggered as I wrestled with a budding thought until it surrendered its lesson. Many more emerged out of conversations and incidents with countless people. This book, then, has come about through their contributions, which enhanced and clarified the final product.

I am deeply grateful for colleague clergy and lay members of the Southwest Texas Conference. So many have been gracious enough to read the weekly—and later biweekly—editions of "Second Thoughts" and to express appreciation for having been humored, challenged or inspired by the text.

It is my sincere hope that the reader will glean from these pages a bit of the joy I have received in writing them.

Blessings and peace!

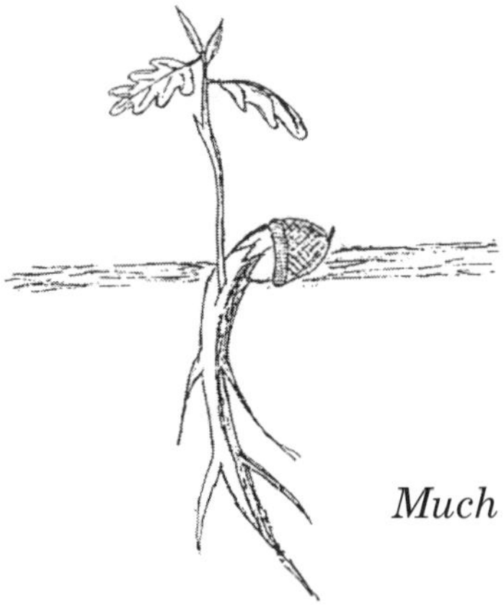

Much is the end of little's faithfulness
Context: Psalms 1:3

Acorns to oaks

"The stately oak tree is but a tiny acorn that held its ground." What a dependable truth: acorns to oak trees! Major ends are frequently the final ends of minor beginnings. As the children's musical *Bullfrogs and Butterflies* puts it, "Tadpoles turn into bullfrogs, and cocoons turn out to be butterflies."

What does it take then for a tiny acorn to become a mighty oak tree? Lots of things. First, the acorn has to carry in its being the germ of a stalwart oak. A thistle can never be an oak tree because the thistle possesses its own possibility.

Second, an acorn must possess an aggressive will to become an oak. No timid acorn ever beat even a bramble bush in its reach for the stars.

Third, it takes toughness for an acorn to become an oak tree—toughness to resist the howling storms that would break its timber, toughness to endure drought that would wither it, toughness to subdue menacing diseases that would stunt its greatness or bring it down to the ground.

Standing its ground, withstanding storms, subduing its obstacles, and through it all, remaining true to itself—that's what makes mighty oaks out of tiny acorns. That's also what makes distinguished heroes out of common folk like you and me.

Baggage is as important as destination.

Context: Psalms 107:28

Airline agonies

After boarding a plane that didn't work recently, we had to deplane to board a working specimen. Of course, the second one was parked at a gate plumb across forever. While waiting again to take off, I met a couple across the aisle. They were adding up frustrations of air travel. All day they had been waiting in airports, trying to get home from a holiday cruise.

Noticeably irritable, the man said, "Baggage service is a joke. We spent all but the last two days of our holiday without our baggage. When I checked our luggage early this morning, I said to the ticket agent, 'Here are our three bags. I'd like one to go to Dallas, one to Denver and one to Seattle.' Dismayed, the agent replied, 'Why, I can't send your bags to three different places.' To which I replied, 'Why can't you? You did it on our way over.'"

Getting luggage to land where you do is an increasing pipe dream. That's why more and more people drag their oversized bags down too-narrow aisles over disgruntled passengers who are stuffed into too-little seats.

One thing is certain. Air travel is getting no better. Knee space is still nil, even on "long liners." Shoulder space is still cramped despite airlines bragging on their "wide-bodied" fleets. Mediocre meals still require squeezed-in, humped-over positions to get at them. And to think we rush right up to pay good money to endure such discomfort, disgruntlement and disillusionment.

"Good buys" often say goodbyes to real value.

Context: Hebrews 12:16

Bargains

It really happened. *The Capitol Times* of Madison, Wis., carried an ad that read: "For sale: one used tombstone. Splendid opportunity for family named Dingle."

Bargains are as abundant as dandelions in the spring. Some are as colorful. Most, though, come with conditions permanently etched.

I was offered a one-acre building lot once at an "honest-to-God" bargain price. Few dollars down; few dollars a month, for a few hundred years. "Friendly neighbors," the ad said. It sounded great. Looked even better—the front view, that is. Backside wasn't shown.

I found out why. The lot was located some 1,200 miles away on the fringes of a long-established swamp. Alligators and water moccasins held title by squatters' rights. Some neighbors!

Indeed, many bargains come with indelibly engraved conditions: No negotiations. "All deeds final," the fine print reads. If your name is Dangle and you buy a Dingle tombstone, you will be remembered as a

Dingle by those who read your epitaph. That's the hidden price of some bargains.

Most of us would be reluctant to admit to buying such bargains. At the same time, few of us would dare deny having purchased a specimen or two, if there is a lick of truthfulness left in us. All of us are prone to snapping up some latest model of a bargain. It seems an inevitable part of growing up. And growing wiser.

If buy a bargain we must, at least let's put our name to it. And confess it. For only then does God have the "splendid opportunity" of forgiving our bad buys.

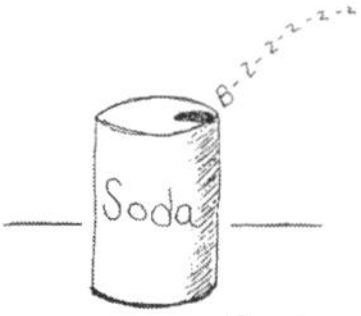

All kinds of bees
tell us the same truth.
Context: Hebrews 12:1-2

Of bees and turtle lips

Nothing is as sensational as the truth!

A close friend came to me recently with an incredible tale about himself. A few days earlier, he was sipping a soft drink from a can. Between swigs, a bee decided to alight and have itself a sip from the same can. It lodged itself on the underside of the top when this unsuspecting friend took another swig. ZAP! Fizzing thunder popped the inside of his upper lip. Then he felt something rumbling around frantically inside his mouth. Gripped with searing pain and panic, he spluttered out the liquid. With it came the soggy and bedazzled bee.

Immediate evidence proved that this sensational tale was true. As this upstanding member put it, "My puffed-up lip made me look like a tortoise. I went around like that the rest of the day–with a turtle lip." Now anybody brave enough to tell such a preposterous tale—and to back it up with evidence of a "turtle lip"—deserves to be believed.

Bees come in assorted sizes and kinds, with hair-trigger stingers. Sin is one kind of bee that always hangs around the edges of our indulgences. Concealed, sin pops up when least expected and where it hurts most. Sin leaves us a "fat lip" of pain and regret. But just as antihistamine counteracts the handiwork of a bee, so forgiveness neutralizes the evidence of sin's designs. We are left with a sharp memory of the sting but also with a caution to avoid the bees of sin that made themselves guests to our indulgences.

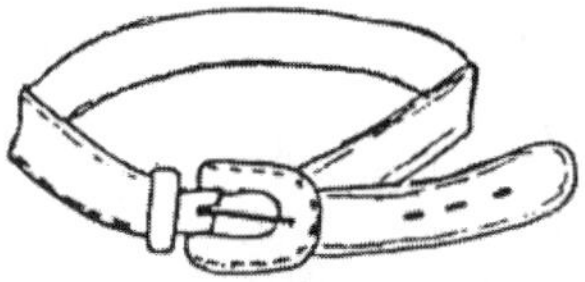

Life is susceptible to all kinds of games.

Context: Isaiah 28:20

Too-long belts

Some of us will do almost anything to make ourselves feel we are making progress with our diet. After several weeks of dieting, one of our fine, upstanding members rushed in excitedly and said to his beloved wife, "Look, honey, I've had to cut off three inches of my belt and punch some more holes in it!"

Eagerly he waited for high praise and compliments. Neither came. Instead, his dear wife replied, "Humph! I know all about those *too-long* belts. I have some of those myself."

There are many painless ways to make you feel good about your diet progress. One is to adjust the scales downward after you step on them. Another way is to wear shoes when you weigh and then deduct twice their weight.

Still another way is to stay off the scales altogether and then accuse yourself of losing a pound a day until you get down to your desired weight. If all else fails, buy a "too-long" belt and keep cutting it off and punching new holes until you trim down to the size you want.

Sound like silly games? Of course! But no sillier than the games we play with our souls.

We pitch God an occasional dollar and then feel good all over with generosity. We stay away from worship and then say, "But I've already been twice last year." We offer hit-and-run prayers and then bless ourselves for being "ceaseless pray-ers." We give two hours work to the church's garage sale and then compliment ourselves for being dedicated.

But whether we play the dieting game with "long belts" or the delusion game with short devotion to God, the result is the same. No flab is subtracted from our bodies, and no nurture is added to our souls. We fail on both counts.

Better is the antidote for bitter.

Context: Acts 8:23

Bittersweet

An old Yiddish proverb says, "Sugar can't sweeten the bitter of heart." Any of us can rake up sufficient reason to become bitter: A lie started on us. Some disappointment. An injustice done to us. Loss of stature and dignity at the hands of someone else. Any of these can turn us sour and caustic.

But difficulties can make us better instead of bitter. Indeed, it has been those noble souls who opted for *betterness* instead of bitterness that have deposited lasting values. Think what would have come about if that maligned preacher of Galilee had responded in kind to his enemies. Consider what our value system would be today if he had not prayed, "Father, forgive them." Think of the blood bath in India had not the last words of a tiny man to his assassin been "I forgive you, and I bless you." Think even what this country would be today had a black preacher rallied millions to take up arms against prejudice instead of calling them to be better in their hours of bitterness.

Few of us will ever influence such millions of people. But the world is still composed of pieces and parts. The extent we become better in our difficult circumstances, therefore, is the degree bitterness is denied a foothold.

Sugar still can't make bitter sweet. Nor can it make us better. But striving to be better instead of bitter is bound to make our personal arena a bit sweeter for everybody.

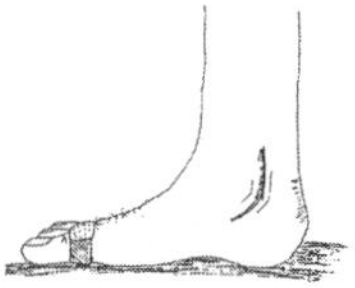

Blisters often accompany blessings.

Context: Romans 8:18

Blisters!

My toe was stinging. I couldn't figure out why. Finally, I investigated. No matter that it was midday and that I was in my office. I removed my shoe. Good grief, there it was! A wrinkle in my sock had rubbed a huge blister. I was disgusted.

Special care was in order, lest I break the bubble and double my misery—to say nothing of having to explain a limp from the siege of pain.

Fretting over the unwelcome nuisance, I was reminded of the comment: "If you want to make a place in the sun, you had better expect some blisters!" Though the words were true, I was in no mood for wisdom. Nor right then was I much concerned to make my place in the sun. I was more eager to take the "sun" out of my throbbing toe.

Blisters, of one sort of another, seem the condition to high achievement. I'm sure Franklin Delano Roosevelt endured many "blisters" as he wrestled with polio and steel leg braces.

I'm sure too, Anne Sullivan must have developed lots of blisters in her life as she tenaciously brought a blind and deaf girl (Helen Keller) into the world of communication and self-respect. Indeed, blisters do seem to be a condition for making one's place in the sun.

Even so, I'm not at all eager to rush out and rub another blister, just to meet the requirement for making my place. Truth is that I'm about ready to scrap even any oncoming renown for present relief.

The sun will come up again tomorrow, and I'll have another chance. Until this blister heals, therefore, I'm willing to wait for my place in the sun.

Bones can verify only that life was lived.

Context: Ezekiel 37:5

Bones

According to legend, Diogenes, the cynic philosopher, was found one day examining a pile of human bones. Puzzled, Alexander the Great asked, "What are you looking for in that pile of bones?"

Diogenes replied, "I'm looking for the bones of your father, but I can't tell them from the bones of the slaves."

Several insights there: Bones can tell us many things about the past. They can enlighten us concerning former civilizations. They can inform us on patterns of human interchange in past civilizations. Indeed, bones can tell us a great deal.

Bones however, cannot tell us whether a person was a Democrat or Republican. They can't tell us whether a person was a Methodist, misfit or mendicant. They can't tell us about personal character or values.

Bones of kings are indistinguishable from slaves. Bones of conquerors are indiscernible from philosophers.

Bones are merely the frames upon which the flesh of life is draped. And it is what the fleeting flesh achieves and deposits that makes the lasting contribution.

Alexander the Great died at 33. At his death, he bequeathed a divided-up world, around which conflict has continued to be the order of the day.

In comparison, a Galilean Carpenter also died at 33. His death became a magnet around which the divided-up world could become one.

Our skeletons discovered centuries from now will not reveal our values. Rather, it will be by which of the two philosophies we have lived.

Love has no ending

Context: 1 Corinthians 13:1-13

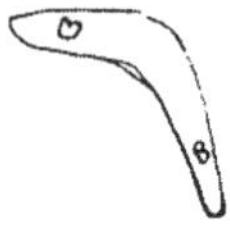

Blessed boomerang

Love is a wonderful game. There are always at least two winners.

In the hallway near the nursery of a church I served was a bulletin board. Pinned thereon were lots of little red paper hearts. Passersby were invited to write love notes on the Valentines.

I liked that. The theme of the bulletin board was "Love is a blessed boomerang."

I liked that, too. Those who conceived the idea and made those hearts available to us must be loving people.

Indeed, love is a blessed boomerang. You cannot distribute love without receiving it back. Nor can you send it out to someone in particular without it touching several bystanders as it makes its rounds.

Unfortunately, the laws that govern the activity of love govern all the activity of its opposites. Just as love on its rounds blesses the heart, so resentment sullies the soul when it returns.

Entertain resentment, and its tutor as well as its

target is damaged. By stoking the embers of our wrath, we succeed only in banking the fires of our impending misery.

Someone said, "True love doesn't have a happy ending because true love doesn't have an ending." It's true. That's why love is so much like a boomerang. Its orbital flight knows no ending. It knows only new beginning.

Checkout pardon delivers the soul, too.

Context: Deuteronomy 6:18

Of milk, muffins and bacon

It's remarkable how little things can come so near to assassinating the soul.

Recently, I had breakfast in another city. A simple breakfast, I thought. "Raisin bran and bacon," I said to the waiter. "And make sure the bacon is crisp!"

As I said, it was a simple breakfast. But everything went wrong.

The raisin bran looked exhausted—with only a nuance or two of raisins. In addition, the milk was stale. Thinking I was decidedly civil, I asked for another pitcher of milk. The waiter glared at me as if insulted.

"Never mind," I said, "just bring me a toasted English muffin instead, with my bacon."

They both arrived in pitiful shape. The muffin was charred in random spots. I concluded it had been toasted with a blow torch. And my "crisp" bacon was both limp and translucent. Grumbling inside, I ate around the charred spots and nibbled the edges of the translucent bacon.

"Check, please," I said icily. It came. The waiter had scratched through the cereal but had failed to add the muffin.

"Well, that's his problem," I muttered. "I'm not going to tell the cashier, either. This place deserves to lose money."

By the time I got to the checkout, my soul was sorely sagging and crying for mercy. I relented. I informed the cashier, lest my soul sour on the spot.

Maybe I'll eat there again someday. But if I do, and the outcome is the same, I'll not go back. I believe thoroughly in "turning the cheek" again and again. But nothing is said about forgiving limp bacon and stale milk and blowtorch muffins served by a glaring waiter.

No best of breed in the human show.
Context: Psalms 8:1-9

Best of breed?

Martha Beckman tells a delightful story of a preschool girl named Marie and her pet collie named Charlie.

One day Marie took Charlie to class as her proud and certain-to-win entry in the class pet show. That afternoon the girl's mother picked up Marie and the collie.

"Well, honey," the mother asked, "how did Charlie do?"

Gloomily Marie replied, "He almost won best of

breed, but at the last minute another collie showed up."

That's about how life works out for humans, too. Many of us would take the "best of breed" if someone else were not always showing up at the last minute. It takes only one other entry to knock us out of the running.

Most of us don't need to look for an array of competition, since only one comparison will do. Indeed, we'd take the prize if there were no one else with whom we were compared.

Yet how we stack up against other entries is never what the "human show" is all about. Every entry is God's entry. In God's scheme of things, there is no "best of breed" mentality.

Therefore, we don't take our self worth from how we compare with someone else. Even what might appear a very best specimen is still sadly lacking when reflected in the mirror of God's hopes and dreams.

We are not collies. Or competitors. We are creatures with God's image imprinted into the texture of our beings. That's what gives us our real value—not how we fare in comparison with another specimen.

Much of our limitation is in our minds.

Context: Matthew 19:26

Of bumblebees

According to the law of aerodynamics, a bumblebee is ill-equipped to fly. The ratio of its body to weight, shape and wingspan simply declare it incapable of flying.

Yet the bumblebee goes right ahead and does it

anyway. Apparently, the bumblebee hasn't been notified of its obvious limitation. Let's don't tell it.

Few scenes are more refreshing than a bulky, black-bodied bumblebee busy about kissing blossoms and coaxing the nectar from their petals. A bumblebee is an industrious creature. It works hard, long and alone. When it departs a blossom, it leaves the observer with an invigorating sense of just being alive.

But there is a scary side to bumblebees. Some of them bore nests into porch posts and header beams. They homestead in unwelcome territory and become irritable when treated like squatters. Pushed to the point of threat, a bumblebee readily vents its ill-temper by depositing a searing sting on the flesh. Though the bitty bumblebee is barely an inch or so in size, it can send a 6-foot-6 he-man scampering for cover.

The bumblebee has a whole lot of lessons to teach us scientifically informed human beings. For one thing, it teaches us never to assume the power and potential of anything by its symmetry and size. But perhaps the most valuable lesson it has to teach us is this: God didn't mis-make us or mis-equip us. So we never know what we *can't* do until we have done it anyway.

No burden is the heaviest burden.

Context: Psalms 55:22

Burdens, boredom and blessings

What is life's greatest burden? Is it disease? Shattered dreams? Broken relationships? Someone else's welfare? What indeed is life's heaviest burden?

An elderly and lonely man was asked that very

question. He replied sadly, "To have nothing to carry." I have a strong suspicion "having nothing to carry" might well be life's greatest burden.

Many of us complain rather quickly just how heavy are the burdens we carry. We count up quickly how many "thorns in the flesh" we are given to bear. We whimper when others load up our lives with their cares. Such burdens certainly aren't enjoyable. They don't make delightful companions for the journey of life.

Yet I suspect life is a lot less meaningful and a lot less fulfilling when we have "nothing to carry." For, you see, life without burdens is soon susceptible to boredom. And that is by far a more subtle and treacherous burden to endure.

As Frederick Buechner puts it, "To be bored is to turn down cold whatever life happens to be offering you at that moment." I'd rather be burdened any day than be bored. A bored life is devoid of anticipation. A burdened life never is. Not only that, but burdens can become blessings. Embrace the burdens others would have you share, and at least two blessings are yours. One, you are apt to be delivered yourself from any lingering source of boredom. Two, you are likely to find your own life made richer. And stronger.

Sleeplessness is sometimes embarrassing.
Context: Isaiah 12:2

Jumping bean burglars

The late Bishop Walter Underwood told the story of a friend who was awakened after midnight by his small child.

"Daddy," the child whispered, "there's someone in the living room."

Groggily, the father replied, "Go back to sleep."

His second child came in and said, "Daddy, someone is in the living room."

Not wanting to appear frightened, the father got up and listened for the "burglar." Sure enough, noise came from the living room.

Cautiously, he crept downstairs. Fearful he might be assaulted, shot or stabbed, he felt for the light switch and flipped it on. The culprits were caught in the act.

On the table was a bowl of jumping beans erratically popping around, causing burglar-like noises. What a chuckle the whole family must have had. All except the father, that is.

A bowlful of unfinished responsibilities regularly steals our sleep. Like frisky jumping beans, those responsibilities keep us awake much of the night. The silent noise they make in our heads convinces us they are much more menacing than they really are.

So we wind up not with stab wounds but with stubbed toes from table legs and door facings we encounter in the half-darkness of grogginess.

A smart way to hush the noise of jumping beans is to put them away safely before bedtime. A smart way to deal with "jumping bean burglars" that steal our sleep is to flip the full light of truth upon them—even if it's 2 o'clock in the morning.

Replays of wrong does not make it right.

Context: Proverbs 14:12

Blushing cameras

Television cameras seldom blink but often have reason to blush. Much of what is offered is but high-class garbage straight from the dumps of human depravity. "We just reflect what the real world is like," a television personality casually remarked.

Hogwash! While some of what is splashed on the screen is happening, it doesn't reflect "real life." By drawing its material from the hog wallows of human degradation, it does say, in effect, "This is the norm of behavior." Television is powerfully persuasive—for good or bad. Thus, if sipping cocktails in satin-sheeted bedrooms of adultery is OK for the "yuppies," it will be OK for the "puppies" of those yuppies.

"Well, you must look at a lot of television," someone is apt to object. Not really. I don't need to see or hear what some middle-aged cutie of a sex therapist says to know what she espouses. After all, I deal regularly with wreckage of life after her proponents have been wounded by her ill advice. I help her disciples work through the debris of their wrong-headedness into forgiveness, dignity and self-respect again.

Most of what television dispenses is not "real life." For one thing, there are never any dirty dishes in the sink of a soap opera. Nor spots on the crystal drinkware. No actors are ever out of sync or shabbily attired. It's just opulence, fantasy and foolishness. Such is a fictitious world that has little to do with the real world. Indeed, even cameras have reason to blush.

Quick checks make lasting differences.

Context: Esther 3:14

All snaps and no shots

Scooping up our two cameras, we headed off to an azalea festival. We wanted to capture the spectacular colors and arrays. I took picture after picture of banks of blossoms. After the 40th "snap," though, I suspected I hadn't taken one "shot."

Horrified at the thought, I sneaked up against a tall bank of azaleas and peaked into my camera. I was being observed. Gleefully, I was asked, "You didn't have any film in your camera, did you?"

Sheepishly, I said, "No," and downplayed my stupidity by changing the subject.

"Surely," I thought, "no one would blab my absurdity." I was wrong.

The first person we met upon our return was told the full story—with lots of frills. For days I endured blushed humiliation as one person after another was told. By the time the last edition was shared, I was barely able to give a tight-lipped grin.

"You can't make a mistake with *this* camera," I was assured when I purchased it. "It thinks of everything. It reads film speed, counts exposures, focuses automatically, flashes if needed and rewinds your film."

I bought the thing with bated breath. But like everything else, it didn't do everything. It didn't tell me no film was inside. Nor did it fail to count exposures that weren't there. Nor did it fail to whine and whine as if it were busy advancing exposures.

I just hope the blasted camera has to suffer as much damage to reputation as I have humiliation.

Like cameras, we sometimes purr and purr and appear to be advancing our discipleship. But what a disappointment God must feel when upon opening our lives, we find we had no film inside upon which his imprint was to be made.

Stupidity usually is the flip side of panic.

Context: Revelation 1:4

Unturned cards

Frustrated, I looked for a stray card upon which I had written an introduction for my next sermon. I thought it was a fine beginning.

"Where have I put it?" I asked myself. "I just had it in my hand! Now it's gone! Vanished!"

Panic struck. For a preacher, losing an idea is like losing a kid. I went through a stack of cards containing related thoughts. "Well," I muttered, "that just beats it."

I'm sure my wife heard my one-sided mutterings and concluded I was talking to the Lord—though the tone and temper of my words must have sounded strangely colorful to be using with God.

"This is ridiculous!" I continued. Again, I went through that stack. Still no luck. I looked in the wastebasket. Nothing there, either. I hadn't even been productive enough to throw anything away.

I got out of my chair, thinking the card might have fallen into it. Still no luck.

I got down on my knees and searched under the desk. I should have prayed while there, for by that time, I needed to. I was about ready to believe God had taken the card because he didn't want me to preach on the subject.

"Well, Lord," I said, "if you are so intent on my not preaching on this subject as to take my card, I'll just find something else!"

Shoving that stack of cards aside, I gathered up a stray card on the other side. As I flipped it disgustedly onto the pile of my now defunct sermon, it turned over as it landed. And there was my "Introduction."

I'm not sure, but I think I heard God chuckle.

"Lord," I said, "Lord, have mercy. I've been stupid again."

And God said, "I know. And I'll probably have to help you preach, too."

And God did.

Time zones are ever changing.

Context: Matthew 6:25-34

Checks, notes and cash

Someone said, "Yesterday is a cancelled check. Tomorrow is a promissory note. And today is all the cash we have, so spend it wisely!"

That's good counsel. Time itself is experienced in three time zones—past, present and future.

Once the check of yesterday is cancelled, it serves only to record what has been. It has no power to add to the account. But it still has significant value. The memory of what is purchased can be both gratifying and satisfying. The cancelled checks of good deeds done yesterday can keep on paying dividends plumb passed today all the way into tomorrow.

As to the promissory note of tomorrow, it is never predated. Its value can be dreamed about today. But no matter what its amount, it cannot be drawn upon until its time is fully come. We are able to realize its benefits only as tomorrow becomes today.

That leaves us to ponder the time zone of today. Indeed, today is all the "cash" we have available. It may seem little or much. Still, it is all we have.

Therefore, we must be careful how we spend it—lest by spending it helter-skelter, we encumber the promissory note of tomorrow. And embarrass the cancelled checks of yesterday.

Contentment is never where you are not.
Context: Philippians 4:11

Contentment

Often contentment eludes us because we think it is somewhere else. Thus, we tend to look for it in wrong places.

I'm reminded of the 50-acre farmer who decided to sell out and start over somewhere else.

A young, bubbly real estate agent came out to get pertinent information for an ad for the farmer's later approval.

Several days passed. No word from the agent. The farmer called about the draft ad.

"I'm working on it," the agent said.

Two days later the riled-up farmer called, demanding to know when the agent would be bringing the ad for him to approve.

"This afternoon," the agent replied. Sure enough, the agent handed the farmer the draft that afternoon.

Unfolding the paper, the farmer read: "Fine 50-acre farm for sale. Well-terraced, fertile land with fenced pasture. Two spring-fed ponds for livestock and good fishing. Tractor and tool shed. Large sturdy barn with hay loft. Two other storage buildings. Also, a lovely three-bedroom home, surrounded by shady oak trees. Lots of romp space for children."

"Well, what do you think about the farm I've described?" the agent asked.

Folding up the paper, the farmer replied, "All my life I've been looking for a farm just like that. I'd be a fool to sell it!"

Two thoughts: One, contentment is most often found right around our feet. Two, sometimes we don't realize just how content we really are until someone else shows us where it is already.

We'd be "fools" indeed to think contentment is any more available where we are not.

Sneezes, yawns and hiccups—kindly reminders.

Context: James 4:14

Control?

Like it or not, life is often unavoidably spontaneous. Much of the time it is simply beyond our control. For example, have you ever tried to cancel an erupting sneeze? Or cut short a surging yawn in mid-gape? Have you ever tried to reschedule a hiccup? We need to be a bit cautious when it comes to spouting off how totally we are in control.

We've all known people who claimed to be on top of everything. They usually come at us with two-legged terror.

"I'm in control of my body!" my First Sergeant shouted in boot camp. "Because I am in control, I do what I want, when I want, as long as I want! And if any of you make it through my training, you too will be in control of your life!"

There I stood, a raw recruit at rigid attention, afraid to breathe lest that First Sergeant object.

"I'm in control of my body," I told myself. And I was, even while a yellow jacket buzzed about my head. "Don't move a hair," I counseled my body. I didn't, until that yellow jacket sat down on my nose. With cross-eyed spontaneity I whisked it away.

Catching my movement, the First Sergeant snarled at me in spluttering outrage, "You are out of control, Recruit!" I knew right then his mother must have been a battle-scarred pit bulldog.

Sneezes don't amount to much. Nor do yawns. Nor

yet do hiccups. But they all laugh at us every time we strut our pompous assertion of being in total control of life.

Trouble is much of our own making.
Context: Psalms 19:12

Get off the cord!

Wendel Fifield tells of an interesting experience. For several minutes he tried to lower the venetian blinds on a large door in his home. He couldn't. Up and down he pulled the cord, but the blinds would go down only part way.

Working up a good case of disgust, he gave up. As he turned away, he realized he had been standing on the cord.

What a parable! At bedtime every night we, in a way, close out the day. We let the curtain down upon another segment of life. But sometimes the "blinds" just won't come down. The day won't close out. Sleep won't come.

We mumble and tumble and grumble our disgust. Finally, we get out of bed and stumble our way to the medicine cabinet for a sleep coaxer. As we swallow down our relief, we are reminded of the reasons the blinds won't come down. We've been "standing on the cord."

An apology due a colleague or employee or friend never got said. So the blind is stuck. A failure of responsibility on our part leaves someone else in a terrible lurch. Or perhaps a lapse of memory of a birthday or anniversary causes us to ignore the event. No wonder the blind won't go down!

We are all prone to stand on the cord. We are all apt to fail and to sport our assorted flaws. But before we get entirely red with disgust for being unable to close out the day, a glance at our feet might help. We just might be "standing on the cord" that lets us slip off to sleep in peace.

Courage is but the conquest of fear.

Context: Isaiah 41:10

Courage

When a seasoned paratrooper was asked how many times he had jumped from an airplane he responded, "None! But I've been pushed 22."

When asked the second question, "Were you scared?" he replied, "Definitely! Every time I was pushed, my mouth filled with cotton. But by the time I landed, there was only the sweet taste of achievement."

It's not always the achievements we reach by "want to" that mark us down as courageous people. Sometimes the weight of a pressing moment "pushes" us to do what we are afraid to do. At other times, circumstances compel us to "jump" into the very face of fear. But once pushed, we are able to look back upon our perch of departure and feel good about what we have done.

I dare say it has been the "push" upon human beings that has shaped our world. Pioneers and settlers all experienced the compulsion to tame this great land we now take so much for granted. And in all instances, they felt the full force of fear, uncertainty, danger. But can you imagine the exhilaration our ancestors must have felt when they looked back upon the "impossible" mountains they had conquered and the "impassible" streams they had crossed?

Life is much a mixture of courage and fear. Each is capable of overcoming the other. But it is when the push of the former overcomes the latter that life for us takes on the taste of triumph.

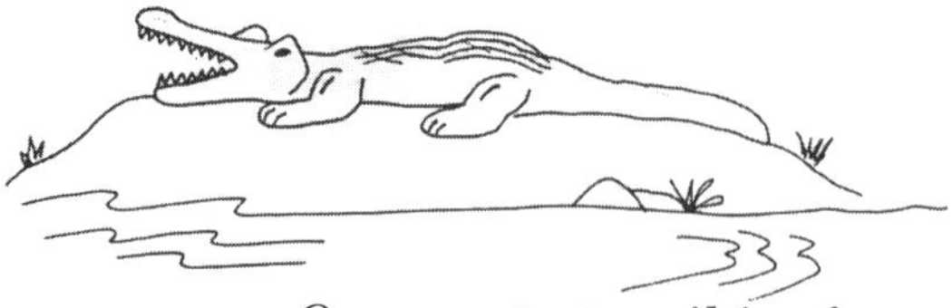

Our greatest peril is often within.

Context: Deuteronomy 20:4

Of insults and crocodiles

While driving from Meru to Nairobi in Kenya, we came to the Tana River. It is noted for its hippo population. I inquired about the hippos and other animals.

My driver-host said, "Oh, many animals besides the hippo thrive along the river." He went on to tell me about the crocodiles and how they lurk in tall grass and shallow water to attack unsuspecting prey.

I confessed to him that crocodiles were not among my favorite animals. "They are scaly of character and grumpy of disposition and ravenous of appetite," I remarked.

My host chuckled and replied, "Never insult a crocodile until you have crossed the river."

I was glad we had just passed over the Tana.

Life is a journey of many rivers to cross. To some

crossings, we bring our own "crocodiles"—e.g., bad temper, selfishness, bloated pride. These, too, slither silently below the surface to imperil us. Or crouch motionless to waylay us in the "tall grass."

We employ many defenses against our personal crocodiles—denial of ownership, excusing their behavior, even fleeing their presence. But the most efficient defense is still the magnum power of repentance.

If when coming to your next "crossing" you find a personal crocodile about to ambush you, don't rile your crocodile with excuses and denials. Own it and repent of it. In so doing you just may render it both tame and toothless. And you are able to pass with peace to the other side.

Intersections: Points of Possibility
Context: 1 Samuel 12:23

Crossroads

In a spasm of honesty, a tired and disillusioned cowboy said, "My life has been filled with crossroads, and I've been taking all the wrong turns."

Crossroads are inevitable. They are inevitable because life is itself a journey. It doesn't flow along pre-planned, uninterrupted routes to some high goal.

Mountains are climbed only by zigzag patterns. Love is achieved only by mid-course corrections of motivation. We simply don't experience life without abrupt and sometimes brutal intersections.

But crossroads are also essential. They rearrange life dramatically. Crossroads are places where dreams are redrawn and destiny is redesigned. They test the mettle of our resolve. They also assess the currency of our motives. They even refine the worth of our visions.

Crossroads then are both inevitable and essential. What we do at intersections, however, is optional. Take a fast lane, and life may well be hurled to lingering regret. Take an easy road, and life may have to settle for a withered substitute.

If the path you are traversing is unpromising, review the road map of your journey. It just may be you have taken "all the wrong turns."

Don't be discouraged. You still have crossroads ahead that can take you where you really want to be. And it is likely you will be joined there by lots of other red-faced pilgrims who also have been on a bad binge. And are looking for the "way back," too.

Sure cures often backfire.

Context: Jeremiah 46:11

Sure Cures

One mule was enough for the farmer who had but a small piece of land. Year after year the farmer and his faithful mule made their modest crop.

One day the mule got sick. His huge head sagged downward. Long ears hung at half-mast. Sad eyes just stared into nothingness. Worried about his faithful mule, the farmer finally called the veterinarian.

"He's just got a severe case of colic," the vet said. "Give him one of these large pills morning and night. He should be good as new in a day or so."

Holding the huge pellets in his hand, the farmer asked, "Say, Doc, how am I to get the mule to take these pills?"

The vet replied, "It's simple. Just take a short piece of garden hose and poke it down the mule's throat. Then put the pellets into the hose and give a quick, strong blow into the hose. The mule will swallow it before he knows it."

The next day the vet phoned to see how the mule was doing. The wife answered, "The mule's fine, but my husband is sick-a-bed and nearly dead!"

"What's wrong with him?" the vet asked.

The wife replied, "The mule blew first!"

Application? Don't try to trick someone else into swallowing your sure-cure pellets for his spiritual colic—or force-feed him some of your well-proved pills. For about the time you get him all primed, WHISH! The "mule" blows first. And you wind up sick-a-bed in terrible shape with a backfire case of colic.

Light is given to illuminate darkness.
Context: Jeremiah 33:6

Cures for no diseases

A budding research scientist came crashing out of the laboratory and into the professor's office. "Professor," he shouted excitedly, "I've just discovered a cure!"

After assessing the student's discovery, the professor replied, "How wonderful! Congratulations! You have just found a cure for which there is no known disease!"

Absurd? Perhaps. Yet more truth exists in such notions than we might think. Take worry, for instance.

Worry is often hurled against calamities that never materialize. Cereals with obese doses of iron are stuffed into bodies whose blood is not "tired." Pills are popped for pains that don't exist.

Illustrious lectures are given on subjects irrelevant. Splendid sermons are preached on issues far removed—or on sins not yet practiced.

I admit to having vacated the pulpit in haste to beat the postlude to the exit door. Occasionally, in the faces of those on the aisles, I've seen everything from blank stares of befuddlement to deep disappointment. By the time I reached the exit door, I already knew I had spoken lots of words that made no connection with their real concerns.

How clever we are at designing and developing solutions for which no problems have been declared. Even sermons, therefore, can be indicted occasionally for exploring in some dark closet for a black cat that isn't there.

Life is a matter of differences.

Context: Hosea 6:1

Sunshine and Desert

"What would it take to make you happy?" the judge asked a troubled young man.

"A million dollars," the young man snorted in reply. "With a million dollars I could put *all* sunshine into my life."

His reply proved only the immaturity and faultiness of his wisdom. "All sunshine" soon makes a desert—whether of sand or a human life. What is meant to be exquisitely delightful for a brief moment becomes excruciating agony when protracted.

A single dish of ice cream is refreshing. A diet of ice cream is quickly repulsive.

Both the bitter and the sweet are vital components to a wholesome life. Pain reminds us of how good life feels without it. Light is never more welcome than when it illuminates the noise in the darkness. Nor is the darkness more appreciated than when it blankets us with sleep. We are never more grateful for heat than when we shiver with cold.

Indeed, sunshine *all the time* makes the desert—just as water unending makes the flood. It takes both in rhythmic proportions to bless life. To enlarge it. To make it whole.

We don't prefer the exhale over the inhale, since both are necessary to sustain life. Would we not then, be wisest by embracing every "beat" as the invigorating prelude to the "counter-beat"?

Who wants all sunshine and a million dollars? Not me. For who wants a ton of money and all sunshine, if he must spend his life sunburned in the desert?

Oneself: the best source for laughter.

Context: Proverbs 17:27

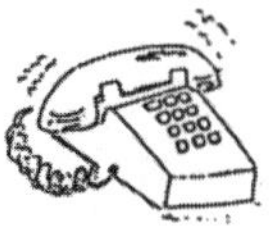

Dialing oneself

Will Rogers remarked, "Everything is funny, as

long as it is happening to someone else." Laughing at oneself is seldom easy for most of us. Yet I suspect oneself is the person about whom laughter is most often merited.

I had a good chuckle once at myself. I had been away from my office. Like everybody else, when I returned, many phone calls were waiting for answer. Other "pressing" matters needed attention, too.

For half the morning I was on the phone. After several calls, I felt some progress. In my hurried pace, I somehow dialed my own number.

When one of the secretaries answered, I was befuddled. Surely I didn't want to ask for me or to talk to myself.

Embarrassed, I hung up the phone, daring not to reveal the caller.

Minutes passed. I concluded the whole incident was a sure sign I was losing it—whatever "it" was. I vowed secretly to keep my blunder quiet—forever. Then I got to laughing at myself. It felt so good, the whole day lightened up a bit.

Some say oneself is the most difficult person to laugh at. Others say oneself is the person most necessary to laugh at. I think the latter is more reasonable. Will Rogers was off base a bit. Sometimes a thing is "funny" simply because it happens to oneself.

Still, I don't plan to call myself again. It may be true "all smart people talk to themselves," but I'd just as soon not have to come away from such conversations having no one to quote but myself.

One destination? One direction!

Context: Matthew 6:24

Revolving doors

Have you ever found yourself opposing a revolving door? I have—just recently. But certainly not intentionally. It was embarrassing and terribly awkward.

Just as I was entering a revolving door into a business, a friend called to me. I turned, as I continued to move toward the door. While I was looking back and walking forward, someone came out the door, spinning it in the opposite direction I had planned. Wham! There I was. Trapped!

I'm sure I was wild-eyed as I staggered backward into the crowded lobby. Those in the foyer, who saw me bumbling my way backward toward them, must have had all kinds of weird thoughts sail through their minds. I didn't try to explain. All the while, my "friend," who had caused it all, was still outside looking bewildered. Come to think of it, it was more the look of denial of even knowing me. He sure didn't hurry inside.

I tried hard to garner some value from that unfortunate incident. I wanted desperately to walk away with at least one honorable lesson from it all. I think I found one. It is this: Life is much like a revolving door. It is designed to admit you into that for which you are created. But don't try to walk through life in opposite directions at the same time. Else, instead of admitting you with dignity into where you want to go, it is likely to deposit you into a whole heap of regret. And unexplainable embarrassment.

Dreams are stronger than achievements.

Context: Genesis 37:19

Achievers and dreamers

Imagination is more potent than knowledge, and a dream is more invigorating than an achievement.

A dream is the stuff of destiny. Any day I'd rather be a dreamer than an achiever. A dreamer is always en route to what has never been. He is always in pursuit of what the rest of the world hasn't thought of yet. Indeed, I'd rather be a dreamer than an achiever.

Achievers suffer letdown once they've passed the goal. "Where do you go when you've won the race? What do you do when the prize is in your hand? What's next when you are at the head of the line, and nothing's there but the top?" Those questions suggest it is better to dream than achieve. For when the trophy's won, the only thing left is to write the memoirs of achievement's great moment.

Not so with a dreamer. Yes, he reaches goals, too, but they are never the end. Achievements are pit stops en route to the unattained. But just as there is danger for the achiever, so there is hazard for the dreamer.

As the achiever's flaw is to stake everything on a single goal, the dreamer's flaw is to tire of the pursuit. In the end, the latter is the greater loss. The loss of an achievement, though significant, is lost mostly to one. But the loss of a dream is a loss to many. Don't let today become tomorrow's yesterday upon which you watch the debris floating in the wake of your deserted dream.

Sowing and reaping. The first brings the last.
Context: Hosea 8:7

Dust devils

Bill and Bob have been friends forever. They greeted me as I joined them for lunch at Rotary. I made a crack about how long Bill had been a member of our church.

Quick as a flash Bob said, "Only the good die young, Ray. That means Bill's got a long time yet to live."

It was a delightful moment, much needed in the middle of another Monday.

Trying to get aboard the high tide of such jesting, I said in faint praise of Bill, "But I have to say Bill is in church every Sunday."

Bob snapped back, "But does it do him any good?"

"Not much!" I replied, "you can't change an alligator's disposition just by preaching at it for half an hour once a week."

Poor Bill. He was amused but squelched. He had endured our onslaught of insults with unusual demeanor.

Down deep though, I knew Bob and I hadn't won. It will take a while for us to reap the whirlwind of our sarcasm, but reaping time will come. When it does, I just hope I am as good-natured in taking it from Bill as he was in taking it from us.

In reality both Bill and Bob are men of faith. They own a track record of strong support and influence in the church. In fact, it was our common faith that made it possible to enjoy each other—at the expense of one of us.

Even so, being "Christian" doesn't shelter us from the returning whirlwinds of our own making. That's why we best be on the lookout with jitters, gazing at the horizon—preparing ourselves to endure with dignity all the dust returning whirlwinds are bound to kick up around us.

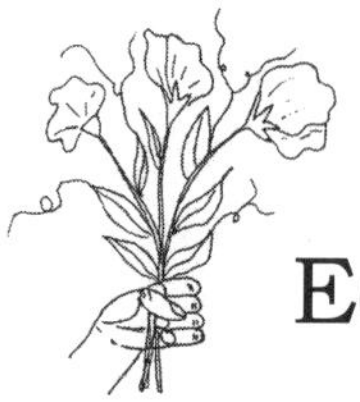

Fragrance echoes, too.

Context: Philippians 4:18

Echo essence

In his book *Jesus Is Calling*, C.E. Matthews tells of a 10-year-old girl who took a fresh bouquet of sweet peas to an elderly neighbor. It was a simple but beautiful act of love.

When she returned home, her mother said to her, "Now dear, sniff your hands." Doing so, the girl caught the delightful scent of sweet peas. Noticing the pleasant look on her daughter's face, the mother then said, "Flowers always leave their fragrance on the hands of those who give them."

So do all the other "flowers" of love we take time to hand out. You cannot give without the fragrance of the gift tarrying to tell on you. You cannot offer a helping hand to someone in need without catching the lingering essence clinging to your hands. You cannot take onto your own shoulders someone else's heavy load and not be saturated with its leftover scent.

Life is much about "giving." Giving presents. Giving cards. Giving expressions of affection and appreciation. Giving time.

But life is much more about "receiving." Not receiving tit for tat. Nor card for card. Nor present for present. It is receiving back from yourself the lingering essence of the gift you have given.

Actually, when you and I give some "flower" of love, we receive back twice: Once from the recipient and once from the gift itself. We receive back gratitude from the recipient of our gift. Then we receive back the wafting, lingering fragrance of the gift itself.

It's a principle of life called "echo essence."

Ego is subtle sabotage.

Context: Psalms 29:23

Bloated ego

Someone commented: "Talent is God-given, so be grateful. Reputation is neighbor-given, so be humble. Ego is self-given, so be careful."

We have every reason to "be careful" when it comes to how much ego we grant ourselves. Regular overstuffing of our ego brings us off looking foolish—sometimes even to those who are supposed to respect us.

A case in point: A bright Army lieutenant was promoted to captain and given command of a company. The promotion was deserved, though long in coming. The new captain felt a swelling surge of ego as he was shown to his new office and desk.

Soon a knock came at the door. Feeling the need to impress the unknown visitor, the captain said, "Enter!" Then he quickly picked up the phone and began to pretend conversation.

"Yes, general," he snapped. "I'll take care of the matter for you right away." Putting the phone down, the captain then barked sharply, "Now, corporal, what can I do for you?"

Looking a bit dismayed, the corporal replied, "Nothing, sir! I just came in to hook up your phone."

It'll do it to you every time. Wrap yourself into a hefty package of pride, and you are liable to look awfully foolish. Grant yourself a bloated proportion of ego, and you are likely to be pitied a bit for making conversation to a phantom on a disconnected line.

Swallowing pride is healthful.
Context: Isaiah 65:5

Swallowing ego

At last Susie had a date with Tom, the most handsome boy in high school. Tom picked her up on time, but Susie came home early.

Surprised, her mother asked, "Susie, you are home early! How did your date go with Tom?"

Susie replied, "Not well at all. Tom may be the best looking boy in school, but he's so egotistical he feels obligated to bow every time he passes a mirror."

Life sprinkled with a dash of ego here and a pinch of pride there is all right. In fact, it is desirable. After all, Jesus said we were to think as much of ourselves as we do our neighbor.

But that doesn't mean we are to love self first, foremost and only. God comes first, neighbor next and then self. Any shuffling of that order so as to relocate self forward leans life downward immediately.

The ego problem with every "Tom" is subtle but serious. If an egotist thought only too much of himself and it ended there, it wouldn't be so bad. But invariably, and at the same time, the egotist thinks too little of others. In fact, the former fosters the latter.

Yet even egotists have some good in them. Few of them are gossips. They seldom go around talking about others. They have so much to say about themselves that they simply have no spare words to speak about others.

Neither is egotism itself all bad. It has proved itself to be both nonfattening and cholesterol free. So, like Tom, having to swallow it at times is quite good for us.

Better fulfillment than success.

Context: Matthew 12:44

Emptiness

When asked why he had become a minister, a pastor replied, "Emptiness at the end of every achievement, and the call of God—that's what drew me into my vocation."

Emptiness is often a sure sign we are living at cross-purposes with God's "call" for us. Yet so many people fantasize, strategize and execute plans without consulting God about God's aspirations for them.

A bright, promising attorney confided to his closest friend, "I don't enjoy being in law. I am a good lawyer, and I'm making more money in my practice than

I ever imagined. But right now I'd like to give it all away for the job I would really enjoy."

When the friend asked why in the world he didn't just chuck his law career and do what he wanted, the attorney replied, "It would destroy my folks. They've sacrificed so much to make me a lawyer. It has always been their dream that I be an attorney."

No one can live life according to someone else's dream—no matter how noble that dream. Nor can the cost of someone else's sacrifice make the dream come true. Each of us has his or her own unique niche to fill. What a waste, then, when that niche is left vacant for the sake of someone else's vision.

Emptiness is bound to be waiting at the end of every achievement when God and the achiever haven't decided together how life is to be expended.

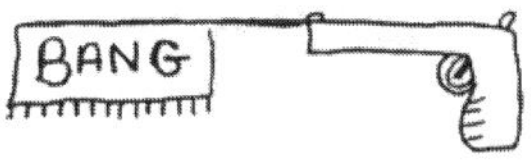

Speed is tempered by direction.

Context: Hebrews 12:1

False starts and dead ends

The race is about to start. Runners are on ready. Feet are dug in. Heads are up, and eyes are fixed down the track. Muscles are taut with anticipation. Ears await the starting gun.

Whoever gets the fast start has an edge on winning. But fast starts are only one factor in winning the race. Direction, too, is vitally important.

Life is much like a race. Many people burst forth with incredible speed and energy. They're off! They get the fast start. But because of faulty direction, they are doomed to lose from the beginning. Their fast start sadly serves as a false start, so the outcome is definitely a dead end.

Judas Iscariot got off to a fast start. He was granted "executive status" as treasurer among the 12 disciples of Jesus. Up front, it looked like he would surely be a winner. Who knows what a noble chapter he might have written in the kingdom's cause had he burst forth in the right direction?

But the bearing of his being was tainted. His fast start became a false start. So he came to a dead end at which stood an ugly hanging tree.

No matter how fast the start, nor how enduringly the race is run, if direction is blemished, the start is false. And the outcome is a dead end. Getting off to a fast start is quite promising. But keeping a sure direction is far more profitable.

Now is forever.

Context: Mark 10:17

"Time for eternity"

It is gratifying to be able to quote the wisdom of our own children. In a recent edition of our son's church newsletter, I was struck by the wisdom of one of his statements. In his pastor's column he said, "Take time to get involved in eternity." What a thought!

Eternity knows neither beginning nor ending. We burst upon eternity without comprehension of where time came from or where it is going. Yet we don't evade the reality of eternity. Our faith in God informs us how we conduct life and toward what ends. That determines the quality of our personal "eternity."

What wiser counsel could we receive then than to "take time for eternity"? Life void of God's influence for the brief span of a lifetime means life void of God forever. On the other hand, life that pays great attention to "forever" exists under the influence of God for the here and now.

And how do we "get involved in eternity"? Surely it relates to our spiritual being. Daily doses of prayer and devotion are a must. Regular worship of God is essential. Loving one's neighbor is necessary. Servanthood is indispensable. Sharing the abundance of what we have with those who have less is imperative.

Such involvement subtly but surely slips us into eternity—until finally we realize that life somehow has become endless.

Wise council indeed, this getting involved in eternity!

No excuse is better than any.

Context: Matthew 19:16-22

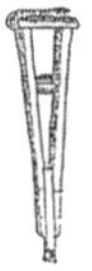

Crutches for lame excuses

"We are all manufacturers," said a businessman. "We are always making goods, making a difference or making excuses." He about summed us up.

Good portions of us are making "goods." We simply cannot live in the world as it is. Put this group into a wilderness, and soon the underbrush turns into home sites. Trees will become houses. Open fire will move into a kitchen stove. The outdoor pallet will relocate to a bedstead and mattress.

Another portion of us is making a "difference." These people won't bequeath to the world only what they found. They have to make a difference for those who come after us. The Edisons and the Salks won't be satisfied until they have formulated for us a better future.

But a large number of us are just making "excuses." We don't clear the wilderness because it would just grow back. We don't cut trees because the ax handle is broken. We don't invent anything because we're not smart enough. Besides, everything worthwhile is already invented.

Excuses are a popular commodity in the marketplace of human affairs. They come in all sizes, shapes and colors. Some are thick with argument. Some are thin of reason. But most are just flabby and feeble.

Whoever designs and manufactures crutches for lame excuses, therefore, is bound to become an instant tycoon. He may even become so wealthy he won't have to make excuses anymore.

Change due only for investment made.
Context: Luke 16:5

Fares with no change due

An 8-year-old but streetwise boy boarded a city bus. For nearly a minute he fumbled frantically in every pocket for the 25-cent fare.

Seeing the boy on the verge of tears, the driver asked, "What's wrong, laddie?"

The boy replied, "I had a half-dollar, but I can't

find it." Touched by the boy's dilemma, the driver paid the fare and gave the boy a ticket. The lad took the stub but kept standing there with his hand outstretched. When the driver again inquired what was wrong, the boy replied, "Where's my change for the 50 cents?"

In one way or the other, most of us have managed to scheme our way into a "free ride." It's commonly known as "hitchhiking." And as if that were not shameful enough, some of us stand around after the free trip, insisting on "change" we weren't entitled to in the first place.

Scheme at it long enough and hard enough, and you can take some good-hearted soul for a "free ride." But in the end, such rides usually prove costly.

For one thing, they rob us of self-respect and detach from us a piece of our integrity. Also, "free rides" seldom deliver us to useful destinations or to honorable reputations. Finally, "free rides" are never really free. They impoverish someone else.

The journey of life brings us to many tollgates. One of the most important gates is our faith in God. What a joy it is to pay the fare!

Look long enough, and you find yourself.

Context: Matthew 7:5

Forgetting faults

After a few months of marriage, a young, brash husband dared to suggest it was time for him and his wife to evaluate their life together. The talk went pretty well at first. That is, until the husband said, "Perhaps it would be helpful if I pointed out your biggest fault."

To which the wife curtly replied, "Never mind! I am already aware of my biggest fault. It is what kept me from doing a better job of getting a husband."

It has always been far better to forget the faults in others—especially in those with whom we expect to associate a great deal. And the best way to forget the faults in someone else is to remember our own.

The human mind is a capricious invention. It can recall complicated details with crisp clarity for decades at a time. Yet it can forget familiar names, numbers and dates within a matter of hours. (Which one of us hasn't had difficulty dialing our own phone number!)

Indeed, the mind can long remember or quickly forget. What it cannot do, though, is remember to forget. The more the mind tries to erase something from its memory, the more it recalls the very thing it is trying to forget.

If we are to forget the faults in others, we must trick our fickle mind by remembering our own faults. That way we do much more good for others and a lot less harm to ourselves.

Rejection is a form of affirmation.
Context: 2 Kings 6:16

Negative favor

A fifth grade Sunday school teacher, noted for being very strict in her class, was taken ill suddenly and whisked away to the hospital. Emergency surgery had to be performed. Everything went well.

Two days later she was sitting up in bed. The nurse brought her the mail, which included a card from her Sunday School class. The card read, "We wish you a speedy recovery." Nine names were scrawled below the message. The teacher was feeling so good until she came to the P.S. It read: "The vote was five to four."

Life seems often up against some kind of vote or another. I suppose we should be grateful that most votes come down in our favor. The vote may be close, but it's usually on our side. For every four who don't seem to appreciate us, five usually do.

I have a dear friend in ministry. We enjoy teasing one another.

Recently, I said to him, "You are a hard man to love."

Quick as a wink he replied, "I know it. But when I get to heaven, there'll be those who love me. They may not be the majority, but there will be a few."

I was outdone again. He was right because there aren't supposed to be any "non-lovers" in heaven!

I hope that Sunday school teacher was not discouraged by her class's narrow vote. After all, the vote did prove no one was indifferent toward her. She was making an impression. And I'd bet any day she'd rather have a "close vote" than be disregarded.

Fear and faith—opposite companions.

Context: 2 Chronicles 20:12

Fear and faith

In a popular devotional magazine these brief words were found: Fear knocked. Faith answered the door. No one was there.

What a message! Though opposites, fear and faith are often operating in the same situation. Fear is strengthened by the absence of faith. Faith, therefore, is fear's sweet remedy.

Fear flows from many sources. It rears its head in the difficulties we face. It unfurls its colors when we are up against the unknown. Fear feasts on many of our experiences. It mingles in our pains. It dabbles in our diseases. It aggravates our confidence. It keeps us on the run from some mistake in our past. Most of our fear can be countered effectively with common sense. Fear of fire is countered by avoiding it. Fear of water is countered by restricting oneself to wading depths. But some fears aren't neutralized so easily. These we must meet with *faith*.

If I rise in the morning fearful of what the day has not yet delivered to me, I can meet the day with faith that the day itself belongs to God. If I am afraid to be myself because guilt is hounding my soul, I can remember that by faith I am forgiven. And free.

It's no disgrace to know fear. What is shameful is to possess no faith. For then, when "fear knocks" and I have no faith with which to "answer the door," all sorts of ogres wait to devour me on my own front porch.

Fear is the invisible enemy.

Context: Proverbs 3:25

Crossed-fingered fear

Jokingly, someone remarked, "In this age of terrorism mentality, greenhouse calamity and diseases like AIDS, the only way to face the future is with our fingers crossed." Those words would be humorous if we could strain out the truth in them.

I suppose every age has had its own set of fears to face. But crossing one's fingers has never been a viable means of fending off fear. Crossed fingers don't nullify a promise. Nor short-circuit some dread. Nor make some wish come true.

Yet many people still sit squint-eyed, with fingers crossed, counting to one backward from 10 in hopes of delivering themselves from some terrible dread.

There is a proven way to face our fears. We take our cue from the life of a common country preacher of Galilee. He had real reason to fear his world and its future. He was a citizen of a nation that sided with Rome against him. He had reason to fear the fierce rejection of his own people in addition to the brutality of a pagan empire. Yet this man lived in splendid calmness and high purpose. Never once did he cross his fingers. Or flinch with fear.

What was his secret? Simple. He knew who he was in all circumstances. He understood what he was to do in all places. He knew who was in charge of his journey and destiny along the way. God was mixed up in all three.

His is the formula quite capable still of delivering us from both the pain of crossed fingers and the fears our crossed fingers can't address.

Remembering is more fruitful than forgetting.

Context: Genesis 41:51

Half-forgetful

Rain was beating down steadily as I got out of my car in the parking lot. I noticed the car nearby had its lights on.

"Someone will soon be stranded by a dead battery," I said to myself. Intending to do a good deed in a hurry, I scurried over to turn off the lights. You guessed it. The doors were locked.

Most of us are only half forgetful. Those who forget to turn off their car lights never forget to lock their car doors. But let's not be ashamed of being half-forgetful. It's still better than being totally forgetful.

Think what would happen if you forgot both to turn off your lights and to lock your car. Some accommodating dude might just open the door and take a seat before turning off the lights. Then he just might hot-wire the ignition and drive off casually with your property.

I used to fret a lot about forgetting certain names, special dates and notable events. I still do. But not nearly so intensely.

"After all," I keep telling myself, "I could be totally forgetful. Then I couldn't remember any of those things. I'd be like that delightful 91-year-old man who complained, 'Well, thunder! I can't recall anything anymore, except what isn't worth remembering!'"

I think I've half-forgotten already all I wanted to

say on this subject. That makes me about average. And puts me in lots of company.

Human: God's funniest creature.

Context: Proverbs 17:22

Funny, funny!

"The longer life lasts, the funnier it gets." You believe that? I do, more and more. The longer I live, the funnier life gets, and the easier it is to laugh at myself.

I drove my car to the sixth floor of a parking garage to an open space. I get dizzy "winding" my way upward to the right for six levels. But it all clears up when I unwind downward to the left to the ground again.

I left my car, took the elevator to the street. Later I returned. Up the elevator I went to the sixth floor and turned right. I reached for my keys. No car! I blinked in disbelief. Still no car.

I began talking to myself, "Where's my car? It's not here! Someone's stolen it! And my new golf clubs are in the trunk! It can't be!"

For several minutes I just stood there pivoting on my left foot, gesturing to myself. Other drivers came by cautiously, wondering why I was turning on my feet, looking startled and talking to myself. Some grinned. I really must have looked funny.

At last I said to myself, "Well, it's just gone. I might as well go back down and call the police."

I pressed the elevator button. No response! Stuck! As I descended the stairwell I said, "Could I have parked in the same slot on the floor below?" There it was.

I began talking to myself again. Departing drivers still watched me talking to myself and looking funny.

Finally it was funny to me, too. But I wonder if I'm going to be able to stand just how funny life is going to get if I last much longer.

Secret giving buys joyous living.
Context: Matthew 6:3-4

Anonymous giving

What a surprise! Someone had sent me an anonymous gift. It was a delightful, yet rather strange, experience for me.

Right off I asked, "Who gave me this?" Mind you, I blurted out this untimely question only seconds after I was plainly told, "It is anonymous." How quickly our reflexes go right ahead and act even when logic has already said, "No need to."

Immediately I began pondering who would give me such an expression of love. For a while I worked on a process of elimination and possibilities. Then I stopped.

"Come on, Ray," I said to myself, "why don't you just accept it, enjoy it and be grateful for it?" From that point the gift took on additional value.

Being the recipient of an anonymous gift is at least a triple treat. One, it makes every person nearby a *suspect* for blessing your life. Two, it makes you want to burst out onto the sidewalk and hug everybody in reach for fear you will miss the rightful donor. Three, it upgrades your own attitude tremendously just to know you are the recipient of someone else's deep appreciation.

I must admit, though, that the anonymous gift has developed in me a new suspicion or two. I suspect in the end that it is the anonymous giver who is the one blessed more. I suspect, too, that the recipient feels so loved he will want to rush out quickly and become an anonymous giver himself. I know I did. And I did.

Anything that could make me feel so good about myself and everybody else, too, is bound to be good for the whole world. So I want to keep this good thing going!

Rejoice today! It's the "good old days" now.

Context: James 4:14

Good old days?

Recently the lights went out at our house. They flickered several warnings, but we ignored them. I went about my sermon preparation when—PLINK—the lights went out. Blackness descended. It was plumb quiet, too.

Calling out to each other in the darkness to see if either of us was doing anything to bring light, my wife, Lavell, and I finally found some matches and candles. Then we came up with a lamp and some oil.

Fumbling awkwardly, we finally got enough light in the den to make a shadow. It was so dim I couldn't even see to write down a phone number from an incoming call. In the midst of our mutual groping Lavell said, "Remember the good old days?" I did. And I didn't covet a single one of them.

We are quick to accuse our yesterdays of being "good old days" since we can look back on them from the safety of today. At no time, however, have I ever thought turning a tap for water today was worse than winding a windlass for water from an outside well on a frigid January day. Never once have I preferred a heat-producing, smelly, smutty kerosene lamp to flipping a switch for brighter, cleaner, safer light. Nor have I ever thought to trade in a self-defrosting, ice cube-making refrigerator for a dank and drippy old icebox.

"Good old days" are just that. They were good when they were happening. But they lose rank rapidly when brought forward. Only today, with all the baggage we bring with it and all the promise God has put in it, is indeed the only "good old day" worth embracing.

Grace is preaching's vital companion.

Context: Colossians 4:6

Grace and gumption

Most of us preachers need a resident squelcher to keep us from taking ourselves too seriously. In most instances the spouse serves quite well in that capacity.

While driving home from worship, a certain pastor was anxious to hear his wife confirm how splendidly he had preached. It didn't happen. In fact, the atmosphere was stiff and quiet.

He had put a lot of time and work into the sermon. He had made a strong delivery. His major points had been clear, even if a bit judgmental. So the pastor waited for some affirming word.

Hearing none, he asked rather smugly, "Well,

honey, what did you think of the message this morning? I, myself, felt it came off rather well." (Strange how most preachers are quick to tell you what we think of our sermon before you can respond to our questions.)

Staring straight ahead, the wife simply said, "Honey, you are not God."

The pastor was stunned. Undaunted, he replied, "Well, I've always suspected I wasn't. I'm glad to have my suspicions verified. And to know all those problems of the world are not my responsibility."

As pastors, we are quite good at deflecting and deflating criticism. We are pretty good, too, at trivializing criticism we don't want to take seriously.

No doubt about it, "we're not God." Nor are all the world's problems on our shoulders. These two facts alone cancel any tendency we may have to be judgmental in our preaching. Or smug in our deflection of criticism from those who love us anyway. And want to see us fulfill our calling with grace. And gumption.

Splinters, though painful, can be our friends.

Context: Acts 2:37

Against the grain

Herbert Farmer once said, "Man cannot go against the grain of the universe and not get splinters." I suspect few of us would want to offer a rebuttal.

The "grain" of anything includes its character, its fabric, its warp and woof. The "grain of the universe," therefore, consists of such things as orderliness, balance and interrelatedness.

We are rapidly realizing how our living against the grain of our world is tearing holes in the ozone, leaving us lethally exposed to death rays. We are realizing also how careless abuse of natural resources is killing our lakes, streams and forests. And their inhabitants as well. These are no small "splinters" our generation is feeling from living against the grain.

But a vital part of that grain has to do with relationships with God and with each other. It has to do with rules that govern our attitudes and behavior. It has to do with being brothers and sisters who love each other enough to see after each other's needs. Go against the grain of those rules, and life turns on us.

To dabble in dishonesty is to watch splinters stab to death our trust of each other. To saturate our bodies with alien substances gives slivers permission to slink away with our health in their grip. To decline God's held-out love is to feel splinters blocking our wholeness.

Indeed, we cannot live against the grain of the universe and not get splinters. But splinters are not enemies—especially when their prick prods us to repentance.

People are strange
but not grandfathers.

Context: Proverbs 17:6

Grandfathers

A certain grandfather developed a splitting headache. His 3-year-old granddaughter sat on the floor playing with an assortment of boisterous toys. The grandfather took the girl on his knee and bounced her into distraction.

Looking up at the grandfather's head, the girl asked, "Grandpa, what makes your hair gray?"

Having a perfect opening, the grandfather replied, "Gray hairs are caused by too much noise in the house."

To which she replied, "Gee, Grandpa, you must make a lot of noise. Just look at how gray Grandma's hair is."

If you want to get a glimpse of a man's life as God must have meant it to be, keep your eye on the nearest grandfather. He seemingly does strange things. Watch him lay aside all the coins in his pocket for a "friend's" piggy bank. Watch him in July buy bizarre toys for "someone special" at Christmas. Watch him as he seems to endure overloads of racket while certain "little people" disarrange the house.

And watch him scurry out the door to the driveway when a certain "visitor" arrives for a few days. No matter if there is sleet, rain, snow or a whole lot of all three. That *really* seems strange when you notice he is wearing absorbent house shoes.

But such seemingly "strange" conduct is really quite normal for a grandfather. It's normal because the grandchild is the third edition of his unrealized dreams. In the grandchild, all his long hopes are yet alive and have a fresh chance for reality.

Watching grandfathers is interesting—perhaps at times even instructive. But *being* a grandfather is best of all. It's just plumb fun.

Gravity pulls up as well as down.

Context: Titus 2:7

Spiritual gravity

My good friend Larry Essinberg once said, "We usually fall the way we lean." Wisdom always seems to come in small packages. Larry's package consists of only seven words.

Lean frequently enough toward some bad habit, and the habit will win you over. Bend your behavior in favor of undisciplined living, and life plummets out of control. Tilt your ambitions toward self, and you fall in love with yourself where the arithmetic of life reads, "one plus one equals one." Incline your energies toward vulgarities and cheap thrills, and life free falls into a garbage dump.

On the other hand, lean life toward God's high purpose, and you fall into fullness of life. Tilt your heart toward generosity, and you fall into wealth money can never buy. Bend your life toward love, and love will rise up to catch you from every direction.

We are subject to spiritual gravity as well as physical gravity. Each puts a compelling pull on all our leanings. The crucial difference is the final end of the pull. Spiritual gravity pulls us down upon our knees to bring us higher. Physical gravity pulls us down to keep us lower.

Indeed, we do fall the way we lean. But we alone still determine for what we will eventually fall because we alone set the direction of our leanings.

Guilt is the forerunner of grace.

Context: Psalms 51

Guilt and grace

Guilt is a powerful force that can make us do strange things. When a wife asked her husband if he realized what day it was, he panicked. Special days whizzed through his mind—Mother's Day, anniversary, birthday, etc. Nothing clicked. But he felt the heavy guilt for not remembering special days in the past.

Mumbling something about being gone a few minutes, the husband rushed right out and bought a dozen roses. Surprised, the wife said, "Honey, you shouldn't have done it. But these roses will make this the best Groundhog Day I've ever had!"

Indeed, guilt makes us do bizarre things. It is also a resident enemy. Left to do its work, it can undermine and maim our sense of self-worth. A certain "revved-up" speaker said to the audience, "Guilt is just about the worst thing that can happen to us!" No, it isn't.

Sometimes we overdo it when it comes to the total matter of guilt. We make it into a monstrous, dirty five-letter word. The fact is that guilt is also a helpful player in the enterprise of discipleship.

Guilt is grace's way of contaminating any pleasure we get out of sinning. Guilt's work, then, is also to make us realize our need for cleansing. If there is no guilt, how can there be repentance? And if no repentance, how can we be cleansed and forgiven? No, the worst thing that can happen to us is not guilt. A much worse thing is to know the reality of guilt but to deny it or suppress it until it embezzles the soul.

"Bangs often become bongs"

Context: Luke 6:38

Sledgehammers

KAPOWWW! There! It's done! Another flea has been smashed! The whole world is better off!

The instrument of death? A sledgehammer.

KERSPLATTT! There goes another gnat! Sledgehammer again. Sure gets the job done. Too well done, in fact. It's called overkill.

Sledgehammers come in many weights and shapes. All are brutal; some are subtle.

Sledges of iron smash with ruthlessness. Weight plus force crushes all resistance.

But subtle sledges are just as effective. Try walking through a supermarket or cafeteria line in pursuit of a single item. The sledgehammer of "overchoice" neutralizes the will to resist buying excessive calories. Sledgehammers made of words are also subtle. Yet they effectively crush human spirit and maim human personalities.

Most of us don't wield sledgehammers of iron as we move about. But under certain circumstances, many of us are quite capable of wielding sledgehammers of words. Devastation in the wake of those is often just as complete.

Have you ever used a verbal sledge to put down some mouthy person who deserved it? Yet you couldn't walk away feeling the least bit better for the lick you gave him/her. The weight of your own sledge suddenly became an unbearable burden.

In that posture only two options seem open. Either you retire your sledge, or you spend the rest of your days on constant lookout for someone else's sledgehammer coming at you!

Handshakes heartfelt are surety bonds.

Context: Proverbs 12:22

Handshake

Recently I had occasion to drive along Magnolia Street in the town where I grew up. It was a bittersweet moment for me. The houses were still there, but the place was different. There was the old Barksdale house, the Everrett place and the Wrinkle home. Once I knew who lived in almost every house. Now I would know only a few, if any.

My father was a self-employed general contractor. I remembered helping him and my brothers paint or repair many of those houses on Magnolia. Suddenly, I realized I never once saw my father sign a contract for a job. His word was his contract. He needed no co-signer to vouch for his honesty. Nor did he require one from a client. No one needed a surety bond from him. His word, symbolized by a handshake, carried the full weight of a signed document.

Never for a single moment have I wanted to go back to the "good old days." But some of those things we left back there were worth our bringing with us into today. The handshake is just one. That is not to dismiss the value of a written contract. Agreements in writing in many ways keep friends from becoming enemies.

Still, straightjacket contracts too often assume the lack of credibility of parties involved. Now even the simplest agreements require impressive credit ratings, character references and a number of legal minds to ponder loopholes.

Handshakes, of my father's sort, left a person with the force of conscience to live up to honesty. Contracts leave a person with the force of retribution. That's like using the threat of hell as the consequence for misconduct against the joy of honesty to keep us from misbehaving.

I'm still for handshakes. At least in some instances.

Heaven, the secret human hunger.

Context: Hebrews 4:9

Heaven

On the marquee of a downtown church were the words: "Interested in going to heaven? Flight training inside."

Nearly everybody you asked would want to go to heaven. Not many, though, would likely be in a hurry to get started. Most Americans would first want two questions answered: "How much is the down payment?" and "How many forms do I have to fill out?" A few soreheads might even want to see the passenger list before making a final decision.

The church has been bold to claim it plays a vital part in getting pilgrims to heaven. Indeed, the church furnishes "flight training" to help us over the narrow, uphill, rocky way. It charts the "flight plan" for the course we are to take. The church even offers a living fellowship through which strangers and enemies learn to love each other enough to want to spend time in heaven together.

Someone appropriately asked, "Why is it those who don't have enough desire to go to church services expect to go to heaven?" I don't know. I do suspect, though, that naturalization papers won't help.

I'm not saying you absolutely cannot get to heaven apart from the church. I am saying the church's "flight plan" is a tested and proven plan. And that its "flight training" has delivered thieves, a few liars and a whole lot of just plain old sinners to heaven's portals.

For me at least then, "I'll stick with the church." Its plan and training beat by far any alternate plans I've seen.

Today is tomorrow forever.

Context: Luke 16:14-31

"This" equals "hereafter"

For several minutes a third-grade Sunday school teacher told the story of Dives and Lazarus. The students sat spellbound as the teacher explained the law of rewards and punishments.

Dives, a rich man, was in torment because of his life of greed and brutal unconcern for the needs of others. On the other hand, Lazarus, a poor beggar, was in heaven because of his loving life.

Convinced she had made her point quite well, the teacher asked, "Now which had you rather be, Dives in torment, or Lazarus in heaven?"

One quick-minded boy spoke up, "Dives in this life, and Lazarus in the next."

How astonishingly do our youngsters sometimes reveal our secret-most thoughts and feelings. We want life both ways. We want wealth, privilege and independence in this life and then heaven for the next. But we simply cannot have it both ways. We can't build our lives here and now around such things as greed and selfishness and then expect eternal blessings to be ours in the life to come.

What we are in this life has an unswerving way of determining what life will be hereafter. We can't play false with fidelity at this moment and then think such behavior won't matter in the next. We cannot inflict our anger on someone today and think its fang marks won't show up tomorrow.

Indeed, the afterlife takes notice of this life.

Holding Steady!
Context: John 10:2

Heroes, sheep and shepherds

The cartoon in a church paper made me chuckle. In the background was a small flock of complaining sheep. Each was voicing an objection: boring sermons, loss of members, cranky air conditioning, etc. In the foreground were two sheep talking to each other.

Scampering hurriedly away from the grumbling flock was a frizzie-haired, wild-eyed pastor. In one hand was a battered shepherd's crook. One of the two sheep was saying to the other, "You've got to admire our pastor! He's quick to leave the 99 to search for the lost one."

There are, I suspect, times when many of us feel heroic. We feel like going out quickly to rescue the whole world. Energy and vitality surge through our entire body. Oxygen abundant seems to activate our brain. Our imagination explodes with all kinds of surprising possibilities.

Then come those times when we feel much more the *object* of heroism. We sense the urgent need ourselves to be rescued. In such moments it might seem just plain pleasanter and safer to abandon the many to look for the one—to grab the shepherd's staff and head off away from assets behind.

But down deep we know heroes are those who never turn tail and run. Heroes stand steady with one hand around the staff and the other firmly in the hand of God.

Being found is better than staying hidden.

Context: Genesis 3:8

Hide and seek

Which of us, when we were children, hasn't played "Hide-and-Seek"? Remember how all the players, except one, scattered and scampered to find some perfect hiding place? To be "it" was to close your eyes, count to a hundred, then yell out, "Ready or not, here I come!"

Depending upon whether or not you were the "finder" or the "found" determined whether your squeals were of delight or disappointment. Of course, every hidden player was bound to be found.

Which of us, as grown-ups, hasn't tried to play

hide-and-seek with God? Though we are never really "hidden" from God, we often let ourselves believe we are. At times we act as if God doesn't notice our hiding ourselves away. At other times, we act as if God is so distracted with weightier matters elsewhere that he never notices our hiding ourselves away. So we scatter into hiding while God is "counting to a hundred."

Eventually, though, we are bound to hear God say, "Ready or not, here I come."

"Adam," God says, "where are you? Eve, I'm coming to find you." In dread, we wait for God to discover us in our most secret hiding place.

Hide-and-seek can be fun, even when played with God. But the fun is never in *staying hidden.* Crouching away in seclusion and aloneness is not enjoyable. The fun of playing hide-and-seek is in being found. For once we are "found out," we can be forgiven. That means we can start fresh and clean again. There is no "fun" in all of life that compares with that!

Not how to, but how come.

Context: 1 John 1:9

How to or how come?

While browsing through a book display, I flipped through several specimens, only to put each one back with quiet rejection. "How to" books overwhelmed the display. Some "How to" volumes addressed needs the world is not even aware of yet. One book in particular caught my eye. It was titled *How to Get the Most Out of Weekend Horseback Riding.*

I said to myself, "Hmmmm! Just what I need.

Church affairs sometimes resemble a horse show." But I put it back, too. After all, I had no horse and no saddle to go with it. Besides, I had to be in church on Sundays.

Since there were no books on how to get the most out of horseback riding on *weekdays*, I kind of felt left out. Just my luck.

About that time, a fellow pastor came up and asked me, "Found anything worth buying yet, Ray?"

I was ready for him. "Nope!" I muttered. "But at these prices I could spend lots of money for a well-bound volume of disappointment." We left the display to the weekend horseback riders.

I suppose "How to" books are here to stay. As long as people are overweight, books on how to lose it will be in vogue. As long as people are greedy, books on how to get rich will be in demand. As long as people feel left out, books on how to be popular will be big business.

The real question of life is seldom "how to" but "how come." How come I'm greedy? How come I'm overweight, etc? Therefore, to be always in hot pursuit of the "how to" is to be always in the chase of yet another "well-bound volume of disappointment."

God holds hope for hypocrites.

Context: Isaiah 9:17

Hope for Hypocrites

At a meeting I attended, a handout was distributed with a cartoon on it. Sitting in his easy chair is a disheveled, unshaven young father, still in his pajamas, reading the newspaper. It's Sunday.

In comes his first-grade son from Sunday school. Immaculately dressed, with Bible under arm, and nose tilted slightly upward toward snobbery, the lad says to his father, "You want to know what I learned at Sunday school today, hypocrite?"

Sometimes, we accumulate just enough religious language to become pious snobs. We just can't wait to try out our lately acquired jargon on someone else's flaws. We just can't wait to pop someone else's eyes into shocked glare with our lethal language.

Hypocrites are plentiful. They live everywhere. Tracings of pretense cling even to the best of us. That isn't to say being a hypocrite is OK. It is to say there are sufficient tinges of false faith in all of us to discourage any of us from highlighting hypocrisy in the rest of us.

Back to hypocrites in the church. They are there. Lots of them. But I have never heard that any spotter of hypocrites improved his own stock by pointing out some shame in someone else.

Besides that, I'm glad many of the hypocrites are in the church. Think what damage would be wreaked upon society if they were all out there on the streets. Inside the church, they at least have a hope.

Right doors are as important as right keys.

Context: Psalms 84:10

Of keys and doors

With briefcase in my left hand and two days of mail squeezed between my body and right forearm, I stood at my study door. My teeth assisted my thumb as I fumbled the key from the holder. I must have looked as precarious as I felt.

It was one of those situations where you can't turn loose of anything. And wouldn't you know it, the key wouldn't fit. Again, I poked at the lock.

"Maybe the keyhole is upside-down," I reasoned. But my upside-down key wouldn't work either. By now, some of the mail was slipping out from under my right forearm. "Nothing's going right already this morning," I fretted.

It was no use. I plopped my briefcase down at my feet. The mail I released into a pile on top of my shoes. With hands now free, I'd get the blasted door opened in a hurry. Still no luck.

"Well, drat!" I snorted. "What's wrong with this key?"

Then I noticed. Nothing was wrong with the key. I was just standing before the wrong door. The "right" door was the garage door at home. How foolish I felt. And how grateful I was that no one was in the office area at the time.

Life often catches us aiming the wrong key at the right door. Yet the key of resentment never unlocks the door to love. Nor can greed open the way to generosity.

Lesson? Before we load up life with excess baggage, which forces us to fumble out the wrong key, let's make sure of the door we would open.

Poison is still "poison" even if the label reads "honey."

Context: Matthew 23:25-26

Of labels and contents

While looking for shaving lotion at a shop in Jamaica, I happened upon a shelf full of all sorts, sizes and scents. As if suddenly seized by gravity, I was drawn to take hold of a beautiful bottle of after-shave cologne. The bottle was absolutely high class. So was the price. I couldn't believe they could ask that much for a bottle of anything.

There I stood, gazing at that elegant specimen of men's indulgence. I had a hard time deciding which was the most attractive—the gold-leaf label or the rippled glass bottle. "The ultimate essence for men," the label read.

"Now that's pretty heavy stuff," I muttered to myself.

I was tempted to take it several times, but recurring jolts of common sense jarred me back to reality. But I simply couldn't resist taking a sneak sniff.

Ugh! It was plumb awful. It was "ultimate" all right, the ultimate mistake for a men's cologne. Gravity released me. I returned it to its place of infamy on the shelf. And left.

On the way out of the shop an old adage came to my mind: "Changing the label doesn't alter the contents of the bottle." I thought, "Maybe not, but that label ought to be changed from 'ultimate essence' to 'final warning.'"

A lingering lesson: Labels are convenient, but they aren't always convincing. In the end, it is the contents inside that determine the integrity of the label outside. And that's true whether the container is a handsome bottle or a human being.

Light is essential
to the blind, too.
Context: Matthew 13:13

Lanterns

Somewhere recently I came across the account of a blind man who was curled up in the sidewalk corner of a building. At his feet flickered a lantern. Though late evening, it was still a curious site.

A pedestrian was intrigued. Pausing, he squatted down and said to the blind man, "Why the lantern at your feet, since both light and darkness are the same to you?"

Turning his face toward the pedestrian, the blind man replied, "It ought to be obvious. The lantern is there so that no one stumbles over me."

How easily we "seeing" people are able to view things from only one angle. We assume everyone else sees things precisely as we do—even those who cannot see. Lanterns for us who live in the "light" are for making our paths plain in the dark. But for those who live in darkness, lanterns are for keeping those who can see from stumbling over those who cannot.

Jesus' words, "having ears you do not use and having eyes you do not see," prove more profound than we realize. Because we are able to hear *everything*, we tend to tune out *anything* we choose not to hear. Because flowers and blazing sunsets are common scenery, we tend not to notice their beauty.

Disparage not, then, the lantern at a blind man's feet. After all, it is not there just for his benefit. It is there for the benefit of stumblers who are supposed to be able to see.

See not only the "lantern," then, but the "light" behind the light.

Direction is as crucial as distance.

Context: Proverbs 4:25

Life leaps

I chuckled at the story. Here came a man crashing down the dock and made a 10-foot broad jump over water to land hard on the deck of a ferry. He didn't land well at all. Wobbling to his feet, he massaged an elbow and several bruises.

A deck hand came right over to steady the man. Puzzled, he said to the broad jumper, "You didn't have to do that. This boat is coming in."

Isn't that just like life? We come crashing down the docks toward the last boat out. Mustering every ounce of energy, we take a broad leap from dock to deck. "KERPLUNK!" We make it. But not without cost. And embarrassment.

We groggily get to our feet to find we have sprained a few joints and bruised several muscles. Then comes embarrassment. We learn we have taken a hard, long leap toward an outgoing journey, only to land on an incoming deck.

A lesson or two seems appropriate. One, don't assume life is always outbound. Two, make sure the direction of your leap matches the direction life is headed. Else your pain is bound to be compounded by embarrassment. Else, too, life looks you in the eye and says to you, "You didn't have to get hurt and look stupid to boot. This boat was on its way in!"

Stop! Look! Listen! Three simple, long-standing words. Yet they still offer sound counsel. Even for people like you and me, who persist in taking outbound leaps onto incoming decks.

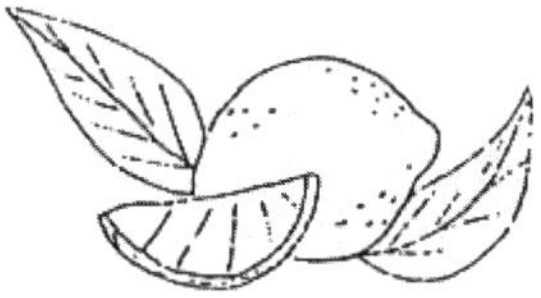

It's what you do with what you get that counts.

Context: Song of Solomon 7:13

Lemonade

"God's Lemonade Stand." That's what the sign read on the store front. You would expect to buy lemonade there, right? Not at this store. Its business wasn't lemonade. God's Lemonade Stand was a bookstore. What a mix of meaning! Or was it?

The owner's motto was, "When life hands you lemons, make lemonade." The bookstore was his way of making lemonade from a load of "lemons" heaped upon him.

None of us avoids an uninvited load of lemons dumped upon us occasionally. Life is too full of diversity for it not to be so. But unpleasant circumstances don't give us permission to curl up in some dark corner of sour despair. Nor do they grant us leave to devalue our future. Sour circumstances can easily serve as fodder for making something useful of us.

Lemons are both good and good for us. But they weren't meant to be eaten as a one-course diet. Lemons offer up their best benefits when they are mingled with other ingredients. It's the same with life. At Calvary Jesus took the lemon of hate and mixed it with love, and the elixir of forgiveness flowed down freely from the cross.

The next time uninvited lemons load up your life, don't panic. Or despair. Or curdle with cynicism.

And don't dive right into eating every last one of them as one-course meals.

Instead, squeeze a few into lemonade. Or grate some into icebox pies. Such mingling of your "lemons" will refresh your life. And put a start back into your soul.

Love is its own homing device.
Context: 1 Corinthians 13:13

Twin longings

For many years a crusty man lived in sullen seclusion. His home beside a narrow gravel road advertised its long neglect. Those who knew the man said the longer he lived alone, the more bitter he became.

One hot summer day a newspaper reporter found himself on that road with a flat tire and no spare. Seeing the man on his front porch, the reporter asked if the man could help. Soon the reporter smelled a human-interest story.

"Why have you lived alone for so long?" the reporter asked.

A bit annoyed, the man replied, "Love flew from this house 25 years ago."

With persistence the reporter then asked, "Who caused it to fly away?"

As if jolted by resurrected guilt, the man snorted, "I don't remember! Besides, it's not important!"

Oh, but it was important! To love and be loved—those are twin cravings of the human heart. Those two yearnings may at times make us do *silly* things, but their absence tends to make us do *sad* things. Indeed, then, it is very important to remember if we are the one who put wings to the flight of love. For "to remember" who caused its flight is to activate its homing device.

"Love bears all things, believes all things, hopes all things," Paul writes. It can withstand anything. Except rejection. Even if it is brutally forced to "fly away," it can fly home again. Even after 25 years. Or 50. All it takes is sincere remorse. And an invitation!

Life is always tentative.

Context: Luke 12:40

Look up!

News of the incident was soon all over town. A falling light fixture barely missed my head and thoroughly disrupted our lunch.

The dining room at the restaurant was full. Suddenly, our plates and coffee were filled with splinters, dust, debris and an assortment of mummified insects. The accompanying crash jarred the entire dining room into shocked silence. Every eye was riveted on our table. A dear friend and I were alive by half an inch. Others at our table were half-dead with disbelief.

Still trembling, one woman from a nearby table commented later, "I saw the fixture coming loose from the ceiling. I tried to yell, but no sound would come out!" How helpful!

Being a firm believer that every experience of life leaves its lessons, I would offer a few hurried ones here. One: Not all descending "light" indeed brings light—especially light from fixtures that make your head their target. Two: If you just have to get attention, do something bizarre. It's safer. And you won't look any sillier than you will trying to gather up dignity after a light fixture, with all its counterparts, settles abruptly upon your meal. Three: Be appreciative when the manager picks up the tab for what you've already eaten. After all, he could charge the falling fixture as exotic entertainment. Four: Don't quit patronizing the restaurant if the food is quality. But do watch where you sit.

Common sense would dictate that you look up at least twice. Once to offer thanks to God for the meal. Twice to make sure no "surprise" is lurking above.

Late is better than lost.
Context: Matthew 25:8-12

Late and lost

When the instrument panel on his private plane malfunctioned, a desperate pilot said to a welcome voice in Tucson, "I don't know where I am, but already I am half an hour late." What a predicament!

In the flow of life, many of us have felt not only lost but late. It's no fun being there. When direction is lost, life crumples up on us rather rapidly. Without definite direction, life is mostly existence in the haze of ambiguity.

A man who had spent half his life wallowing in waiting thrills confessed to a friend, "To this point my life has known more adversity than adventure." Nothing surprising there. Such is bound to be the eulogy written across any life spent in random ramblings. Meaningless meanderings can never be a worthy substitute for the high adventure we are created to experience.

More than a century ago a wise man said, "Men, like nails, become useless when they lose direction and begin to bend." Still true! We cannot amble aimlessly through life, granting every wind permission to bend us as it pleases.

Ancestors who gave our world its shape may not have known at all times just where they were. But they must have been sure of where they were going. If we would shape the world we pass to our heirs, we must be no less sure of our direction. Else we might wind up in the awful plight of that pilot—both lost and late.

Luck is the offspring of vision and labor.

Context: Psalms 73:26

Luck

I chuckled when my usually upbeat friend said to me gloomily, "I'm so unlucky. If I broke my leg, I'd get crutches too short." He went on to say, "Even the artificial fruit on our coffee table is beginning to rot."

At one time or another, I suppose all of us catch a case of black-dog-blues about how life is treating us. In the throes of such misery, we tend to blame our circumstances on the lack of luck.

I wonder! What is luck, anyway? One world political leader in the 1940s defined luck as "being shot at without results." I'm not at all sure "being shot at" could be classified as luck, regardless of the "results."

After more than half a century of living and learning, I sense life is not much a matter of luck. Some, perhaps, but not much. There are usually reasons when life is bandied about by some unexpected or unexplained "fortune." As someone put it, "A rabbit's foot is always a poor substitute for horse sense." How can a rabbit's foot have anything to do with luck when it so obviously didn't work for the rabbit?

Bad judgement played out is far more likely to bring bad results than bad fortune. So is sound planning carefully performed far more apt to bring pleasant ends.

Choice, not chance, then, is far more likely to determine the outcome.

Frivolity can contain value.

Context: Proverbs 4:7

Mall mania

While browsing in a super-mall, I encountered things I didn't know the world needed. Having survived aisles and piles of gimmicks and gadgets, along with curios and keepsakes, I was drained.

It's hard on one's constitution to be subjected to so much "you gotta have this!"—especially when you're not exactly sure what it is or why you need it. I felt like the mountaineer, who having visited a supermarket, said, "I ain't never seen so many things I could do so good without."

Yet one plaque in that place plagued my mind. Etched into a cedar slat were the words, "Weekends, Paydays and Vacations—That's What I Live For." Perhaps my trip through that mall of mania had not been a waste after all.

Are "weekends, paydays and vacations" what we really live for? I fear that for many of us, it is truer than we quickly admit.

Weekends serve as time zones for our planned distractions. Paydays are the means by which we don't quite finance them. Vacations are all too often our excuses for getting away from it all. Just what we are trying to escape is not always clear.

But what if we add spiritual value to each? What if our weekends became time zones for spiritual renewal as well as physical distractions? What if paydays served as the means also by which we put God first in our financial affairs? And what if vacations were spent "getting unto God" as well as "away from it all?"

That would give real currency to that cedar plaque. It would make it worth purchasing and hanging on a conspicuous wall. And reading every day.

Speak clearly; God is listening.

Context: Genesis 11:1-9

Second meanings

Much of our language comes with second meanings. When a little girl asked for a compass in a dime store, the clerk asked, "Which kind, the one that goes places or goes in circles?" Confused, the girl burst into tears and ran out the door.

Life is complicated enough without coming at people with second meanings. Very easily can we make our words mean what we don't say.

"Some friend!" we remark. Right away the listener hears second meanings. Do we mean a valued companion? Or an enemy? Or is the reference to some kinky relationship?

No wonder governments have difficulty communicating. Think what it must be like for officials using a language with "second meanings" to understand each other. It's no surprise that "difficulty in translation" is so often the scapegoat for broken pacts and agreements. Perhaps it was a good idea after all to implement "many" languages at the Tower of Babel. At least there, people spoke "one meaning" words so clearly that God could tell their conduct was unbecoming. I'm not sure even God could do that so easily today. The tower fell because their words were so clear they *exposed* their wrongdoing.

It's a crazy world. Like compasses, our words are always taking us to strange places or taking us in circles. And the predictable consequence is the same: Confusion. Or wrongdoing. Or both.

Miser is but four letters from miserable.

Context: James 5:3

Miser-able

I had to chuckle recently when someone said, "Some people are so tight-fisted that if they pay you a compliment, they demand a receipt." Are there really people like that? I hope not, for that's about as far as a miser can go and hope to come back.

I've met some pretty "conservative" people in my lifetime. Several thoroughbred models of misers have crossed my path. I've encountered a few who definitely were not afflicted with generosity. But so far, I have not met a specimen so tight as to ask for a receipt for a compliment given. I don't think I will, either. For you see, no miser is apt to dole out his compliments any quicker than he is his cash. Not only that, misers are far more likely to deal in complaints, carpings and criticisms.

The word "miser" is but four letters away from "miserable." That's no surprise. If you are the *first*, you will soon become the second. Of all the unhappy people on planet Earth, misers must compose a large group. They seem to have so few friends. Except, of course, those of like stripe. Yet because of their mutual affliction, even their friendships must be more surface than substance.

Also, misers never have "enough"—either to give or to enjoy. Their outlook is simple: Spend or give as little as you can to get back as much as you can.

Though I don't recall being given profuse doses of compliments by misers, I'd like to be. Giving lots of receipts would have to be loads of fun.

Conviction strengthens; compromise weakens.

Context: Proverbs 16:25

Mocktail

"Mocktail." New word! Old ploy.

Time was when a drinker darted off the street into some dark bar to take a quick and secluded swig. He was deliberate to appear not to be a drinker. Somehow he felt it more honorable to be a non-drinker. How things are changing.

Now it is the teetotaler who often feels a bit excluded. But have no worry. Now the nondrinker can casually stroll into a bar, take a seat and swig a "mocktail," while giving every appearance of sipping a cocktail. The mocktail is designed for those who want to look like they are imbibing, when actually they are not.

On the news recently a woman in a bar said to a television camera, "With a mocktail, I don't have to feel left out. I can be one of the crowd without being a drinker." What ingenuity!

What a shame to become a part of a group you don't want to belong to in the first place! More important, what a compromise of character!

Perhaps it really is true we will do almost anything to be accepted. But if we compromise conviction to identify with practices we conscientiously disapprove, we flaw ourselves dangerously. In time, either conviction breaks down or compromise sells our souls.

I think even God at times must get confused with all the games we play. At least, God must grow weary at our efforts for appearance's sake. But thank God, God is God, whose patience with us outlasts all our silly shenanigans.

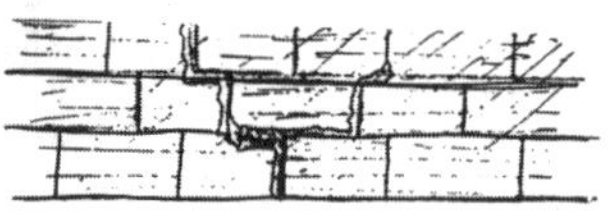

Glue is more important than glamour.
Context: Luke 6:47-49

Dishonest mortar

In 1906 one of America's worst disasters occurred. An earthquake took several hundreds lives as it reduced San Francisco to wreckage and rubble.

Following that awful tragedy, a study was made to determine why so many stately buildings collapsed so quickly. It was concluded that many of them crumbled because of "dishonest mortar."

No matter what lofty-appearing lives we build and no matter the pedigree of each brick we put into the make-up of life, if the mortar is "dishonest," life is bound to collapse. The integrity of what holds all the contributing parts together, therefore, is of utmost importance.

While the guest of a church in a community, I was told about the town's "likeable failure." It was said, "Jim could have been a governor or senator. Everybody likes him immediately. He could have been a fine physician or professor, for he certainly has the intellectual ability. He could have been anything, had he not persisted in hanging his life on a lie."

I never asked just what that "lie" was. Nor was I ever told. Whatever it was, however, it served as the "dishonest mortar" that reduced Jim's life to the sorry stature of "likeable failure."

Within our grasp are numerous materials with which to mix the "mortar" of life. Be careful, then, what ingredients you select—lest having built a stately looking life, you see it collapse under the siege of some moderate earthquake.

The best is often the least.
Context: Luke 19:17

Missing the most

"I never really looked at my roses," a rose grower said. "I was always primping them for show. I watered them with precision. I measured their food and fertilizer. I sprayed them with care and groomed them of every flaw. I displayed them with profession.

"Yet in all that, I never really noticed their matchless beauty. Then at a rose show where I had won the grand prize, my best friend said to me, 'Fred, I want you to look at your winning rose. Really take stock of its shape and symmetry. Look at its colors. Touch the texture of its velvety petals. Then breathe into your soul the delight of its fragrance. For once in your life, Fred, enjoy what you have spent your life missing.'"

Sound familiar? Like Fred, many of us are unaware of what we are missing, even though we live very close by. But whether we miss out because we are "busy," "diligent to our goals" or just an "intense person," the results are no less unfortunate. We still miss the abiding value of simple things like a rose.

An old adage says, "Don't forget to smell the roses." It's good counsel. But just "smelling" isn't enough, either. We need equally to "feel," to "observe" and to gather in the deeper fragrances life offers. And most of all, we need to pause frequently to thank God for giving us senses to perceive the simple riches of God's handiwork. In so doing, our lives are more apt to become examples of beauty and instruments of value.

"Can do" follows "have to."

Context: Isaiah 41:10

Mountains

On a mountain in Korea is Kwang Ju Temple. It houses one of the largest statues of Buddha. A Korean friend talked me into climbing the mountain to see it.

It seemed exciting. Halfway up the mountain trail, my excitement quickly faded. Farther up, I began to tell myself I really didn't want to see the statue. A bit farther up still, I simply declared I couldn't go on. All the while, lots of Koreans were passing me upward on the trail.

Several stopped, bowed, smiled and encouraged me to keep climbing. My friend, Kim, said to me teasingly, "You can make it! I believe in you! Besides, you have to make it! You are an American. Look how big you are up against all these small Koreans who are passing you."

It wasn't "small Koreans" I was up against; it was a steep and rugged mountain. But their encouragement and Kim's teasing did reinvigorate me. I felt compelled to make it to the top.

It's never the "size" of life, the degree of our toughness nor the karat of our pedigree that makes us strong. And keeps us climbing our mountains.

It's usually the encouragement of others and their unflagging belief in us.

Peter's denial of Jesus had utterly exhausted and defeated him. But then Jesus looked at Peter. And in that look Peter heard Jesus' silent words, "I believe in you, Peter. So you can make it up this mountain, too!" He did! And so can we.

Some news is too true to be good.

Context: Proverbs 17:9

Celery and bad news

Some time ago, the *Wall Street Journal* depicted a doctor saying to a patient, "First the good news. You can have all the celery you can eat."

Celery is certainly good. And good for us. But having "all the celery you can eat" sure isn't "good news" if it is *all* you can eat. That suggests an interesting conclusion.

Sometimes the "good news" we give—or get—is really "bad news" that is used to introduce even "worse news." It's like standing on a neighbor's porch and saying, "First the good news. I didn't run over your dog, but it died instantly of fright." No good news there in either case.

Seize the initiative the next time some eager friend runs up and says to you, "I've got good news and bad news." Right there, you should say to him, "Gimme the bad news first. I don't want it to wind up worse news by having it pass through the strainer of good news."

You are apt to realize at least two rewards if you

seize the initiative. One, you are likely to startle the bearer of "good news" so thoroughly that he will forget what the bad news was. And both of you will benefit from that. Two, if you short circuit his "good news," then he has no means to introduce the bad news. So he has no news to bring. And we all know that no news is good news.

Confused? See how well it works already.

We cannot go where God is not.

Context: Proverbs 3:6

North to right

What a small world! While in England, my wife, Lavell, and I met a couple of fellow travelers from Georgia whom I had worked with on a mission in Australia. We had a joyous reunion.

After a bit, we got onto the subject of our sense of direction. Rosalie said humorously, "I have absolutely no sense of direction. Every way is north to me, and I like to turn right."

Poor soul! I tried to help her. "Don't you even know where the sun sets?" I asked.

"Sure!" she replied. "It sets at the back of our house."

I had no will left to help her.

Flickers of spiritual insight flare up even out of lighthearted conversation. We are all traveling somewhere. When our course is God, therefore, any turn we make will be "right."

God is at the far end of every personal tragedy. He resides along every lonely lane. When dark despair manhandles us, God's presence surrounds us. Morning or evening, uphill or down, every way we turn is "right" because God is the end of our travel.

It's valuable to master which way north is from south and east from west. But it's far more valuable to point life steadily on God. Then it will not matter which way the wind blows, the sun sets or the moon rises. For always we will be turning homeward to God.

And like Rosalie, in a sense, we can blurt out in confident joy, "Every way is God, and I like to turn right!"

Life is face forward, always.

Context: Hebrews 11:8-10

Nostalgia

Last summer my older brother and I visited the home site where we lived when I was a preschooler. My first memory as a child began there.

The old house was gone, but the lay of the land was familiar. I could visualize where the house had been. As we stood on the gravel road looking into the overgrown site, both of us were struck suddenly quiet. It seemed appropriate.

For the first time in my life, I knew what it felt like to say, "Sixty years ago,...." It was a strange feeling. My soul was stirred as I saw again our family in our early years. I had a yearning to slip back into a half century ago. Then I shuddered at the thought of going back to where I was first aware of life.

Someone said, "Nostalgia is longing for a place you wouldn't move back to." It must be true. As precious as my memory is of those earliest days of life, I wouldn't move back. Like it or not, life always faces forward.

A flashback visit, therefore, is quite enough. There is that irresistible pull that brings the face forward again to where we've not yet been but must go.

I don't think life is a face-forward proposition by accident. It's an inborn, spiritual compulsion. We are pilgrims on a journey into untraveled horizons. We are possessed by a yearning to realize that for which we are created. That knowledge is never behind us.

It's probably good to take a quick trip into where we came from. But we're never permitted to stay there. The heavy pull of tomorrow is ever upon us, turning our faces forward to what we fully are.

No part is small in God's agenda.

Context: Matthew 25:35-36

Small parts

Charles Brookfield, a former actor, read a mistaken newspaper report of his death. He knew he wasn't dead, for he could hear himself reading the startling news out loud.

Gazing eyes shifted to a gaped mouth as he read the rest of the report, which summed up his acting career. The report ended by saying, "Though Brookfield was never a *great* actor, he was invaluable in small parts."

Most of us would probably stand alongside Brookfield if we could read *now* a summary of our lives.

Few of us would rank among the "greats." And that's OK. For it is by playing "small parts" well that leads to greatness.

George Washington Carver became a "great" by excelling in "small parts." Carver confessed that when he was a young scientist, he prayed pompously to God, "Lord, I want to know all the mysteries of the universe."

God replied, "That's fine, George. But the universe is a little much for you. Here's a peanut. When you've mastered all its mysteries, we'll go from there."

Carver took that peanut. For years he probed its majestic mysteries. And somehow, Carver got marked down among the "greats."

Watch those newspapers! If you should find your own death reported therein, you have a right to be startled. But don't be as concerned about being dead as about how well you have excelled in the "invaluable small parts" assigned to you.

Paths are seldom easy,
but nevertheless necessary.
Context: Psalms 25:4-5

Paths

"If you find a path with no obstacles, it probably doesn't lead anywhere." It's fascinating how another's thoughts trigger vivid memories of one's own past.

Paths played a big part in my boyhood days. We beat paths to lots of places—especially in summertime when short pants were the uniforms of the day. We pounded out paths to "swimming holes." We laid down paths through the woods in search of hazelnut bushes. We made slick trails to our hideouts. Paths were roadmaps. If I knew which one a friend had taken, I knew I could find him.

Our paths led past challenging places. Some took us down into deep gullies and up steep embankments. They led us across rippling brooks where slippery rocks and water snakes made our passing precarious. Occasionally, they took us through patches of pungent, bitter weeds and blackberry bushes—both of which left our bare legs and feet stinging.

I recall how, after traversing some arduous path, we would return home. Our brows would be brimming with sweat, which descended in rivulets to form "dirt beads" around our necks. Fifty-five years haven't dimmed my memory of those special days. Nor washed away the sense of achievement for having made the trip over one of those trails.

The paths we travel as youngsters are much like those we travel as oldsters. The only difference is the values of what the paths lead to and how much effort we are willing to spend to overcome the obstacles along the way.

Virtue does not point out its lack in others.

Context: 2 Corinthians 6:4

Patience

Patience is a peculiar virtue. It cannot be stored away for some special occasion. It must be put to regular use, or it is of little use.

Frustrated, a young mother went charging into

the back yard. For the third time in a single hour, she untangled her son and a neighbor boy. They were in the full swing of boyhood combat...again!

Yanking one boy to his feet with her left hand and the other boy with her right, she shook them until dust fogged from their clothes. "I've had it with you two kids," she screeched. With that, she stalked back into the house muttering premeditated child abuse under her breath.

As she banged the door shut, her husband looked up from his newspaper and said rather smugly, "Sue, where is your patience?"

Still steaming, she bristled at him, "I'm saving my patience for a rainy day! Why don't you go out there and use up some of yours on those kids?"

How quickly do we notice the absence of some virtue in someone else's life—especially when it's not our turn to account for the depleted stock of that same virtue in our own lives.

Pause long, then, before you would take stock of someone else's short supply of virtue—lest you, like that husband, be invited to go out immediately and use up some of the supply of the same virtue you seem to possess in such abundance.

Hypocrisy comes in many chic forms.

Context: Galatians 6:7

Clay pearls and impotent yogurt

Speaking of her costume jewelry, a prominent actress said with a tinge of mischief, "There isn't anything more fun than wearing something and having someone assume that it is real when you know it's not."

For several days I pondered that actress' words. "Surely," I said to myself, "her words don't accurately state our values today." Then later, while standing in line for a cone of yogurt, I read an echo of her words.

There, on the wall, was a dazzling picture of a huge yogurt delight with all the "impotent" trimmings. Underneath the picture were the words, "All the pleasures and none of the guilt." Everywhere we look these days, signs and symptoms of subtle hypocrisy abound. Fooling others seems indeed to be an increasingly popular pastime. More and more we fool people with clay pearls and then call it "fun" when they are embarrassingly deceived. We gorge ourselves silly with "pleasures" and then promptly declare ourselves exempt from any guilt.

Eventually though, our upside-down values must come right side up. Inevitably, we get what we plant—good or bad. Only in multiplied proportions. Beware then of delighting to sport clay pearls and of feasting on impotent yogurt. Neither is likely to turn out fun. Nor leave us guilt-free.

Securing the pen is as
vital as refilling the ink.
Context: Matthew 12:44

Of pens and ink

In all my years of writing, I have never run out of ink at a convenient point. Pens are bound to go dry in mid-sentence—or during some vibrating train of thought.

While at my desk recently, ideas and thoughts rushed in to compete for expression. They came faster than I could write them down. It was exciting. That is, until that dry scratch on paper. Out of ink!

Hurriedly, I separated the pen to replace the empty cartridge. In one hand I held the pen part, with the other the expended casing. I rummaged the drawer for a refill and had difficulty locating one.

The delay was stealing the voltage from the thoughts I wanted to get down. By the time I found a full cartridge, I couldn't find the pen part.

"Well, foot!" I said. "What have I done with the pen?" For several minutes I bounced about amid the fine steam of disgust. The wastebasket was unprepared for my assault. I manhandled it, accusing it of kidnapping my pen. All the while, I clutched that infernal empty cartridge in my hand. Having disemboweled the wastebasket of its crumpled contents, I spotted the pen. There it lay, at the very bottom, as if mocking me. By then, all my glorious thoughts were long departed.

"Sometimes," I wrote later, "we get so enchanted with our own genius that we ignore how dangerously empty of God's 'ink' we are becoming. From that point, it is rather easy to displace, by distraction, the very source we must have, if we would write out God's dreams for our lives."

Pessimism and persimmons are double cousins.
Context: Job 10:22

Pity the pessimist

The late Gerald Kennedy told of a certain pessimist. Every day he catalogued his objections.

"The whole world is gone to the dogs," he whined. "No hope."

He viewed the future through the bifocals of pessimism and persimmons.

Trying to solace her grumbling father, a loving daughter said, "Cheer up, Dad. You could be dead, and then all your troubles would be over."

Unmoved by his daughter's insight, the man snorted, "Not so, daughter. If I were to die tonight, it would be my luck to be resurrected in the morning."

Don't chuckle too quickly. How recently has it been since you were the one to highlight the dark side? We are all prone to practice the art of pessimism at times. Some are more "prone" than others.

About the only thing some people ever get excited about is the future. They can hardly wait for tomorrow so they can look back on today with regret. It's hard for some people to see the good because their antenna is tuned only to static. For them, the glare of possibility burns so brightly they squint their eyes and see only gloom.

Any day I'd rather be an optimist than a pessimist. I'd rather look for the best in someone than search for the worst. It's better for the soul to see a glass half full of apple juice than to call it half-empty.

What is the cure for pessimism? Suprisingly, the pessimist himself gave the answer. It is "resurrection." Resurrection with *new* eyes for *new* days. It, too, is God's gift.

Oozing or choosing: our daily dilemma.

Context: Numbers 13:32-33

Squatters or pioneers

H.G. Wells tells of a conversation of two men at the Colosseum in Rome. Said one, "Think of the men who have stood in this place." The other replied, "Think of all the men who will."

Two conflicting views of life rise out of that conversation. One view dwells on what has been; the other view dwells on what can be.

Perhaps a more familiar way of pointing up these conflicting views is that of squatters or pioneers. Squatters exploit what others have built; pioneers sacrifice to build for the future. Squatters are always digging in; pioneers are always moving out. Squatters tend to leave others alone; pioneers try to bring others along. Squatters are head motivated; pioneers are heart motivated. Squatters concern themselves with the practical; pioneers concern themselves with the possible.

Squatters become what they are by oozing; pioneers become what they are by choosing. Because squatters don't aspire to fly very high, they are bothered by pioneers who do.

Peter Marshall once observed, "As you look at Grandfather Time, you cannot tell if in his hand behind his back he holds a bouquet or brickbat." Maybe so. But you and I can tell at any moment in life whether we shall be squatters or pioneers.

Which, then, are you fast becoming—a squatter or a pioneer? You need not answer with words. What occupies your life will tell. Are you occupied, then, with trying to tame down geysers or trying to occupy mud holes?

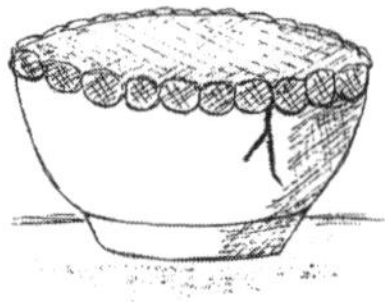

Perfectly loved but not perfectly made.

Context: Ecclesiastes 3:11

Cracked pots

Some time ago I read a delightful book. One chapter was titled: "You Are Only an Earthen Vessel, but God Has a Market for Cracked Pots."

When my eyes fell on that title page, I just knew I was going to enjoy every word of that chapter. I did.

Before we get very far into the aging of life, we make the essential discovery that none of us is perfectly made. Nor perfectly promising. Indeed, we are "earthen vessels" with glaring chips and chinks.

What we amount to in life, therefore, is never determined by how glaringly flaws pockmark our makeup. The crucial thing is that God has a market for "cracked pots" and imperfect people.

As a boy, I knew a man who loved gospel singing. He would walk five miles each way to hear some gospel group sing. At worship, he would join loudly in the hymn singing. But his voice was plumb awful. The discordant sounds he hurled into the congregational singing sounded like they came fresh off a rusty washboard.

But that man was a marketable product. He could whistle in perfect pitch. Birdcalls were his specialty. When he whistled, the birds paused to drink into their souls his version of their own music.

I'm a pot. You're one, too. We're both "cracked" a bit, which is OK. At least we are always in the majority. Besides that, we can always count on God to maintain a market for each of us.

Priority often points to potential.

Context: Matthew 6:31

Priority and potential

"We know our priorities; we don't know our potential," said the teen-age speaker to the Executive Committee of the World Methodist Council. His words seemed appropriate for his tender years. But as I reflected, I realized his words were fitting for any age group.

Priorities are rather easy to know. Not so with potential. Again and again we are surprised at the potential that resides in any given situation.

At age 22 with diploma in hand, we are apt to see our priorities as finding a job, charting a career, falling in love and succeeding in our dreams. But not many at 22 or 82 are able to realize the full potential of each passing circumstance. Potential is likely to come in tidbits.

Yet there is a rhythm that plays between priority and potential. Peter's priority was to be the most noted fisherman of Galilee. That priority fitted him for his potential to fish for human souls.

Paul's priority was to rid the earth of Christians. That played into the hands of his potential to gather gentiles into the Kingdom of God.

The priorities of these two giants served only to reveal their inner potential.

Indeed, "we know our priorities; we don't know our potential." Yet if we dare set the right priorities, we are apt to realize our God-given potential.

Look long at what appears to be easy.
Context: 1 Corinthians 10:12

Pushovers

Two men walking their dogs met on the sidewalk. Stopping to greet each other, one man said to the other, "Say, that's a mighty mean-looking dog you have there."

The other man replied, "Yeah, and he's every bit as mean as he looks."

Just then the dog lunged against the leash. Breaking free, he tore out toward a much smaller dog in a nearby yard. A terrible dogfight broke out. Petunia petals flew high as dust boiled amid the snarling and snapping. The whole neighborhood rushed out to investigate the ruckus.

Abruptly, the fight was over. Low-eared and limping through the dust, the dog moped back to his master. Panting and humiliated, he plopped down gingerly at his master's feet.

The dark silence was broken as the first man chided, "I thought you said that dog was every bit as mean as he looked."

The owner replied, "Oh, he is! Trouble is, he's a lousy judge of dogs."

We're all afflicted with warped and bloated judgments. We rush right out to take charge of some pushover challenge, only to come back brutally beaten. And bedraggled by the fight we assumed was a snap. I say "afflicted" because we never seem to learn that the size of the challenge has little to do with the "fight" hidden away therein.

In the sting of humiliation and defeat, we seem to learn. But not for long. For soon, there stands another pushover near a new petunia patch, which we feel obliged to tend to so easily. And the lesson is on all over again.

Standard of living and quality of life are not natural enemies.

Context: Luke 12:20

Standard or quality?

Which would you choose: standard of living or quality of life? Both are important. Either is an asset. Neither is dishonorable. Each delivers a sense of well being. Which then would you choose?

Standard of living is geared to creature comforts, material plenty, financial independence and individual security. It is "personal" directed.

Quality of life is "principle" directed. It has to do with a sense of contentment, inner peace and strength of character.

The former indicates what one does for his life. The latter points to what one's life counts for.

I vote for quality. Why? Because I knew a man

who had a marvelous standard of living. His home was a grand residence. He owned more land than you could drive around in an hour. For several days in a row, he could have written a check for more money than the church's annual budget. Any "thing" he wanted could have been delivered to his doorstep.

Yet he was a troubled man. Lonely. Surly. Alcohol gripped his will. He trusted no one. What "friends" he had felt his constant scrutiny. One friend did muster the nerve to say to him, "Jess, if you would liquidate some of your standard of living in pursuit of quality of life, everybody would benefit." Courageous counsel!

Standard of living and quality of life are not natural enemies. But we can make them so. A sure way to make them friends is to sacrifice a chunk of standard in pursuit of quality. It works every time.

Free throws and rebounds. That's life.

Context: Luke 24:13-15

Free throws and rebounds

"We get what we put into life. And that's the trouble!"

Agreed!

Life is much like basketball. It includes a lot of free throws and rebounds. The quality of what comes back is only as good as what is sent forth.

Life is also like planting a crop. If we cast wheat upon the ground, we can expect to get wheat back. But only if the seeds we cast are viable. And only if we prepare the field. And only if we fertilize the soil. And only if we protect the tender sprouts from enemies like cockleburs and Johnson grass. And only if we harvest what we plant.

Nothing is gained until we gather in the "rebound" of our "free-throws."

The same principle is at work in our walk of life. What we put into that walk is what we can expect to get back. Bring shallow, half-hearted commitment to that walk, and we seem much of the time to walk alone. Bring to that walk a hurried and scurried schedule, and God's influence is quite ignored. Bring to that walk loyalty to every little event and affair of the world, and God is soon excluded. But bring undivided love and unflagging devotion to that walk, and everything turns on the axis of that walk. God becomes alive and active in all our other walks. And works. And wonders.

Indeed, "we get what we put into life." Free throws do determine rebounds. That's the trouble. That's also the opportunity.

Remedies are often ruthless.

Context: Jeremiah 33:6

Home remedies

Home remedies are sometimes worse than what they cure. How I used to revolt when my mother got down that big brown bottle of cod-liver oil. It was her remedy for everything from a sour stomach to a warped attitude. We had to take a dose three times a week.

I remember my first spoonful. Choking my mouth

open, my mother said to me, "The first dose is the worst."

She was wrong. Only on those words did I ever question her truthfulness. The "first" dose wasn't the worst dose. The worst dose was the *next* one.

The severest of child abuse in those days had to be a dose of cod-liver oil. It was the gosh-awfulest agony any mother could heap upon her child. That was before courts would charge parents with mistreating a child. Had courts been sympathetic, I think I would have turned in my mother. And gladly would I have furnished the bottle as "no return" evidence.

One morning, before a "dose of death" was due that afternoon, I begged my mother to let me spend the night with a friend. She consented.

"Boy, oh boy!" I rejoiced "I've outsmarted her!"

I hadn't. When I returned home the next afternoon, that ghastly bottle and spoon were on the table waiting to gang up on me. Since I had missed the day before, I had to take it two days in a row. Cod-liver oil had even come between my best friend and me!

Home remedies are usually harmless—except when applied to the soul.

Neither life nor death is left to luck.

Context: John 5:28

Resurrection

Grump, the cranky hermit, made his way to his cabin in the pitch darkness of the countryside. Piercing bolts of lightening promised a furious storm. Faster and faster Grump walked until he was trotting into the driving wind. The only way to beat the oncoming storm was to cut across a large rural cemetery.

Barely able to see the ground, he struck out in the general direction. Crashing jolts of thunder aggravated his skittish anxiety. Suddenly he stumbled and banged his head on a large, low hanging limb, which flipped him into a freshly dug gravesite. All night long he lay unconscious and motionless at the bottom of black solitude.

Daybreak stirred him with strange sounds wafting on the wind. Wobbling to his feet, he peaked cautiously over the mound of dirt alongside the open grave. As his bleary eyes met the rising sun, a mighty shout of singing broke from the one-room churchhouse. "Up from the Grave He Arose!" came the festive lyrics.

Grump looked about his surroundings. He rubbed his eyes, cleaned out his ears and shook his head in utter bewilderment.

"Glory be!" he shouted. "It's resurrection day, and I'm the first one up!"

No such resurrection, for several reasons. One, none of us will "stumble" into eternal life. Two, we aren't likely to be "bewildered" upon arrival. Three, we aren't apt to be the "first one up."

The grave is real. So is resurrection. No surprise, then, either way.

He who has less often has lots more.

Context: Luke 16:18-24

Rich by less

At one time Howard Hughes was among the richest men in America. He wasn't noted, though, as a man who honored God much with his wealth. Some say greed was known to have called a shot or two in his business dealings. His vast fortune wound up in interstate litigation, which at times resembled a circus more than a court of law.

On one occasion a common laborer is reported to have said to Hughes, "I'm richer than you are, Mr. Hughes."

Amused, the billionaire replied, "Oh! How can that be?"

The laborer answered, "Because I have all the money I want, and you haven't."

Many times he who has less actually has a lot more. Noted Christian missionary E. Stanley Jones was on target when he said, "There are two ways to be rich. One is by the abundance of your possessions; the other is by the fewness of your wants."

It isn't impossible or impractical to be richer than a rich person by fewness of wants. How valuable are our efforts, therefore, to do without what we don't need.

Someone told of a very poor man who put up a stranded traveler overnight. Showing the traveler to a pallet in a spare room, the host said, "You are welcome here. If there is anything you want, just let us know, and we will come show you how to do without it."

In most instances, it is in the "getting along without it" and the "fewness of our wants" that we are actually richer than the rich.

Life is ever vulnerable; it need not be risky.
Context: Acts 15:26

Resident risk

Someone posted a sign in an obstetrics floor of a hospital that read, "Recent research shows that the first five minutes of life are very risky." Underneath someone had added, "The last five minutes are not so hot either." Both are probably true.

We struggle to catch life for the first five minutes. We fight to keep life the last five. Whether we are arriving or departing, therefore, life is indeed very fragile and risky.

The hidden blessing at either end is that we aren't aware of the risk involved. Life is handed to us without our consultation. It is taken from us without our consent. Both are consequences of someone else's decision.

But birth and death aren't the limits of high-risk zones. The fact of the matter is that life is pretty vulnerable much of the time in between. At any moment, we are but a few heartbeats away from death.

While the first five minutes and the last five minutes may be "not so hot," everything in between is about "as hot" as we endeavor to make it.

To a great extent, we determine just how risky life is from birth to death. If we put God first, neighbor next and self last, we will still be vulnerable. But risk is minimized. If, however, we diet on such alien foods as anger, greed or jealousy, we will still breathe. We will still traffic in the affairs of life for maybe 90 years. But we will be "alive" only for that portion preceding the diet.

In the meantime, we will exist under double risk: mangled meaning and embezzled destiny.

Deaf ears do hear.
Context: Proverbs 20:12

Ears, eyes and risks

Two prominent dignitaries were attending a high-level meeting. They were in deep conversation when Sir Winston Churchill came in and took a seat just two rows ahead. Immediately, the depth of their conversation shifted to shallow water.

"There's Churchill," one said. "They say his health is failing rapidly."

The other "gentleman" sadly replied, "Yes, and they say he is growing quite senile to boot."

As Churchill departed, he paused, leaned over and said to the two men, "They also say he's hard of hearing."

How easy we find it to confess in secret all the failures of others. We seem to have no difficulty in reciting the full repertoire of their faults. But in doing so, the depth of our own character shifts immediately to shallow water. Not only that, but so often our eager "confessions," spoken so cautiously in secret, are overheard by the very ears of the one who is supposed to be "hard of hearing."

To speak fluently of another's shortcomings is to run two very serious risks. For one thing, such speaking is *prima-facie* evidence that you yourself are well familiar with those very sins. For another, it is to become known as a person with a tragic eye defect, which renders you able to see only the imperfections in others. Caution then—lest your "private" listing of another's sins be the catalogue from which your own blemishes are ordered.

Rocks are also stepping stones.
Context: Psalms 32:7

Song of rocks

Somewhere I read: "The brook would lose its song if you removed the rocks." That's not only a statement concerning brooks, rocks and rills; it's also a statement about life itself.

Certainly, the reality of rocks isn't to be taken lightly. They can be treacherously slippery, which causes us to fall. They sport their jagged edges to injure our feet and ankles. Their hard surfaces invite bumps and bruises.

Yet it is still the rocks over which we thrust much of life that put zeal, flavor and color to living. It is our journey over the rocks, too, that makes us stronger people. And wiser people. And more aware of what life is all about.

What would life be like if there were no rocks in our path? What would happen to us if we refused to walk the way of rocks?

I don't know. But I do have a suspicion or two. I suspect we would feel safe and comfortable. And grow flabby of spirit. And cautious of life. And perhaps a bit surly of soul.

But most sadly, I suspect we would lose many of the stanzas that make life sing. Like a rippling brook with the rocks removed, everything would flow smoothly. And quietly. And probably peacefully. But there would be no harmony or melody to put music into our steps. Or cadence into our strides.

A rocky road is seldom enjoyable to traverse. But in the end, it is preferable. Most any day, I would prefer the rocks to the loss of song in my soul.

Recurring duty is the seed of success.

Context: Nehemiah 13:13

Routine

At his retirement banquet, a labored and effective pastor said, "Every day for nearly 40 years I've rallied around the routine of ministry." His was no small assessment of his life.

Some folks have been known to curse the routine because of its humdrum monotony. Others avoid it as dull waste of time and energy. Still others claim its value and embrace it as the building blocks of long-range achievement. In the end, routine is but the daily deposit we make to the account of productive living.

Few things are more routine for a preacher than preparing sermons. This task means writing, writing and more writing. Just for the fun of it recently, I decided to estimate the number of words I have now inscribed on paper. I included only "finished" words such as those in sermons, lectures, books, articles, etc. I was astonished to discover I have on record well more than a million words. Be advised herewith I didn't sit down and count each word. I leave that to anyone wishing to challenge my estimate.

Several things happened to me upon discovering how many words I have put into final form. For one thing, I realized why my second finger keeps a callus on it. Two, I was both humbled and grateful. Three, I was reminded of the great value of "rallying around the routine" every day. In the future, I'm less likely to grumble about the routine of my calling. In fact, I'm more likely to claim it as a sacred ingredient to productive ministry.

Not "what" but "who" rules your life.

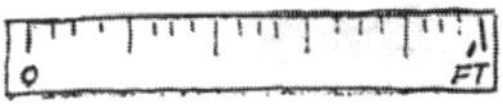

Context: 2 Corinthians 10:12

Rulers

When a lively young boy told his mother he was eight feet tall, he was scolded. "Shame on you, Alvin," his mother said, "you are exaggerating again!"

The boy persisted. Jumping up and down a bit, he said, "But it's true! I am eight feet tall! I am! I just measured myself with this little ruler I made!"

It's an age-old tactic to measure yourself by your own ruler. And to jump up and down a bit to sound more convincing.

Lots of rulers raise their hands for permission to be the standard by which we measure ourselves. Success is one. Many people have called themselves "tall" because of the success they have achieved. Security is another. Some people declare themselves individuals of stature because they have attained some sense of security. These are but two rulers among many whose hands are always raised.

But, in time, life itself is bound to call their bluff. Self-made rulers are never accurate. They take on exaggerated value when measuring self. Six inches easily become a foot. Not only that, but self-made rulers are always subject to self, thereby disqualifying themselves as trustworthy standards for measuring self.

How "tall" we think we are, then, or how tall we want others to believe us to be is of little importance. What is important is how we measure up along the ultimate ruler. That Ruler measured himself so lowly that he surrendered himself to a cross. And in doing so, he made us a bit taller than we could ever deserve to be.

Failure is the running mate of success.

Context: Hebrews 12:1

Self-made

Two men chatted during their 25th high school reunion party. "I went on to college after high school," the first man said, "but my college experience was a disaster. I failed everything but nuclear physics."

Gingerly, the second man responded, "My goodness, that's a tough subject. How come you didn't fail in it?"

"Because," replied the first man, "I didn't take nuclear physics."

There are only two ways to fail. The first is to come up short on an honest effort. The second is never to make the effort. The latter lingers longer with greater grief.

I think it was Lincoln who said, "It is better to try and fail than to fail to try." In the same view Elbert Hubbard said, "There is no failure except in no longer trying."

Surely, it must be more rewarding to "run for the gold" and miss it than never to have trained for the possibility. What if Simon Peter had not dropped his nets and walked away with Jesus? Failure blotched his life with regularity. He blurted out infantile insights. He conducted himself with adolescent bravado. He disowned his Lord. Yet after every failure, he picked himself up, brushed off the dust of his self-inflicted humiliation and fell into the ranks again.

More than we realize, our "effort," or lack of it, *makes* us what we are. The title "self-made," then, is more tellingly and brutally applied to the "failure" who never enters the race than to the "failure" who comes up short in the running.

Many stumbles are over self.

Context: Ecclesiastes 2:4, 11

Tilt toward self

"I want less work to do," an employee demanded. "And more time to get it done! And more money for doing it!"

Typical! Everything seems to tilt toward self almost anyplace we look. It seems to be an inborn flaw. Time was when at least a part of one's motivation for working was gratitude for having a job and the satisfaction of doing it well. That's scarce reasoning anymore.

Most of us are easily enticed into thinking we are quite a bit more valuable in the workplace than we really are. What a jolt, then, when abruptly we learn the world won't fold up and surrender if we resign.

I was amused recently by the sage words of a colleague. Apparently, he had just endured an encounter with a rookie pastor who was top-heavy with self. "Sadly," my colleague said, "he's so green he doesn't even know what he doesn't know."

It's humbling enough to discover just how much we have yet to learn. It's downright unfortunate not even to know enough yet to realize what we don't know.

Life may indeed be flawed with an inborn tendency to tilt toward self. Even so, there's just got to be more to a job than demanding less work to do, more time to do it and more money when it's over.

The trouble with this inborn tilt toward self is that when it finally collapses, self is the one who suffers the initial humiliation. And the lasting hurt.

Shadows are revealing.

Context: James 1:17

Shadows

"Much of the time now I feel I'm living in dark shadows." Those were the words of a seasoned leader who was up against a draining midlife struggle.

We start out in life with a full tank of vim and vision. We leap every barrier in a single bound. But in time, our leap gets lower, or the barrier gets higher.

Or both. Then come those creeping shadows.

Shadows are foreboding. Sometimes ugly. Often scary. But as surely as we live, they will fall across our lives. Like it or not, shadows mire us down to our kneecaps, where we are subject to fall apart at the seams.

More often than we realize, though, shadows are a good omen. They prove the light is still shining. Shadows are sure evidence that the light creating them is stronger than the shadow itself. In reality, shadows serve to reveal the object that overshadows us. And once we know what the shadow is showing us, the shadow itself is tamed.

To dodge daily every shadow is to live life in retreat. To fight shadows with raging ferocity is like shadowboxing: It works us into a heavy sweat, but it doesn't get us very far in the end.

When shadows fall, remember: The light that still shines makes the shadows evident in the first place.

Simple things need little improvement.

Context: 2 Corinthians 1:12

'Coons and simple things

Legend has it that Daniel Boone was escorting a government dignitary through the wilderness. It was in the dead of winter.

Watching Boone's famous coonskin cap whipping in the biting wind, the dignitary said, "Seems to me your cap would be a lot warmer if you'd turn the fur part to the inside."

Politely, Boone took off his cap, turned it inside out, and placed it on his head again. After a few minutes, Boone chuckled out loud.

"What's so funny?" the dignitary asked. Boone replied, "Aw, I was just thinking about that poor 'coon. What a fool he was all his life not to know a simple thing like that."

Sometimes our unsolicited, hair-trigger wisdom turns out itself to be pretty stupid. It might sound reasonable that a 'coon would stay warmer if he wore his fur inside, but there would be serious consequences. For one thing, he'd tickle himself into insanity from an itch he couldn't scratch.

Too, as a bald-bodied, nude 'coon he'd quickly lose all respect from his fellow forest creatures. But most serious of all, he'd probably become a split personality. He'd have great difficulty determining whether his rings of fur inside made him a 'coon indeed or if his bare hide on his outside made him something else.

In most cases, simple things are best left to their simplicity. Lest in applying our uninformed wisdom, we find our own common sense turned inside out.

Sin ever lurks at our door.

Context: John 8:11

Lost sins? Never!

The "Stations of the Cross" has proved to be a splendid spiritual journey. It is a re-enacted, nine-station walk with Jesus from Pilate's court, where Jesus was condemned, to Calvary, where he was crucified.

At one station, the participant is given the opportunity to write down on a piece of paper some of his "private" sins. At a later station, the paper with sins written on it is to be nailed to a rugged cross as a reminder that God has forgiven the participant.

As a lovable couple named Andy and Bailey approached the station where the sins were to be nailed down, Andy became a bit fidgety. Rummaging through his pockets, he said rather frantically, "Bailey, I've lost my sins."

It was a refreshing statement. But Bailey knew better. After all, she had been his wife for nearly four decades. His "sins" hadn't taken leave so easily. Nor disappeared so quietly. But even Bailey could not tell if Andy's panic stemmed from *losing* his sins or from someone *finding* the paper and knowing whose sins they were.

Sorry, Andy! It's a comforting thought. But our sins are never lost. They can be kept invisible by denial. They can be held secret by cover-up. They can be misplaced for a season. They can even be blamed on someone else.

But they are never "lost." They are still hanging around, breeding a whole new clan to plague us.

So to Andy, and to each of us as well, Truth says, "Yours sins are never lost. But they can be forgiven and forgotten. They can be forgiven and forgotten as each day you place your sins on the cross and nail them down with the hammer of Jesus' words: 'I don't condemn you. Go, and sin no more!'"

Almost good is still bad.

Context: 2 Corinthians 1:12

Smokeless smokers

Human ingenuity has done it again. This time it is a smokeless cigarette. It's still white and has all the ingredients for maintaining addiction.

What an invention! Just think! Now you can sit by a smokeless smoker without his exhaust fumes bringing tears to your eyes, sniffles to your nose or nausea to your stomach. Ashtrays will be obsolete, where used gum once spun off interesting fumes from crushed out cigarettes.

I wonder how many "smokes" one smokeless cigarette will contain. Perhaps there won't be any more packs of 20. A smoker can just go into a store; say, "Give me a cigarette"; and pay a dollar for an all-day delight.

As breathtaking (pun) as the invention might seem, I'll bet it doesn't work out. Too many objections. How long do you think tobacco growers will sit still for nicotine being mass manufactured? And what will the government do with all that tobacco subsidy money?

Poker players, too, are going to be outraged. Think how ridiculous six poker players around a table would look twiddling their chips and sucking silently on white tubes. Bic flickers will be out of business. Their instant lighters will be instant losers, to be discarded while fully loaded. Clothiers especially are bound to grumble. Think how many jackets, neckties, skirts and suits are going to be suddenly saved from irreparable burn holes.

Smokeless cigarettes just show us how intent we are at preserving our perversions. And to dress up our own self-destruction.

Life labors to hymn rhythms.

Context: Psalms 23

Soul sounds

The late Archbishop Temple related an interesting incident in his life. It occurred while he was an overnight guest of a prominent family.

From the kitchen the next morning came a servant's lovely voice singing, "Nearer, My God, to Thee." The archbishop, assuming the hymn was being sung for his personal benefit, was so pleased. "What a lovely voice," he remarked to his host.

"Oh yes," came the reply. "That's the song she sings when we are to have boiled eggs for breakfast. Three stanzas for soft boiled and five for hard."

Most of the splendid things we hear and experience are not solely for our "personal benefit." Even so, it's not a bad idea to play the labors of daily life by the tunes and rhythms of great hymns.

In my own life, I have been held steady of spirit by singing Spafford's hymn, "It Is Well With My Soul." I have found new clarity of direction as Charles Wesley's great hymn, "Spirit of Faith, Come Down," seeped its way into my soul. I have felt cleansing of sin by applying Isaac Watt's immortal hymn, "When I Survey the Wondrous Cross." And how many of us have been brought to the starting gate of a new beginning by John Newton's immortal hymn, "Amazing Grace, How Sweet the Sound."

Such sounds bouncing around in our souls can call the cadence in our daily walk with God. So whether you are boiling eggs or building dreams, let their rhythms freely flow!

Simplicity usually is the most revealing.
Context: Luke 2:6-8

Downsizing the spectacular

Do you remember what unbridled pride we all felt when our astronauts landed on the moon and returned? Most of us who were young parents at the time knew that spectacular event would figure significantly into the future of our children.

Joseph Sittler comments on how he felt as his teen-aged son watched the televised moon shots. He said, "I was simply stunned by the magnificence of this achievement of landing a man on the moon! My kid sat there; he didn't even take his feet off the table. He noticed I had my jaw hanging out, and he said to me, 'Don't worry, Pop, they'll make it.'"

Especially since that day, our kids have become so accustomed to so much that they are quickly able to downsize the spectacular we think so remarkable. Toys for our tots consist of computers that draw, spell, configure equations and talk—all at the same time. Mutated space creatures implant basic physics and geometry into 3-year-old brains.

No wonder our offspring are easily able to downsize the spectacular.

I suppose it is good that our children be not so intimidated by their sensational future that they retreat into the security of yesterday. But it would be especially tragic if in their insatiable hunger for more and more "spectaculars" to downsize, they think to devalue the simple ingenuity of God—ingenuity that was born to peasant parents and wrapped in swaddling clothes.

The simplicity of that magnificence defies downsizing.

Kindness is sometimes hard to dispense.

Context: Proverbs 15:23

Speeders

"Firsts" really do happen. I witnessed a "first" last week. One of those 18-wheel trailer trucks on an interstate highway had been pulled over for speeding. The officer was writing out some kind of ticket. Only a few miles earlier, that same rig had zipped passed us at very high speed.

"Well, what do you know," I said to Lavell, my wife, "miracles really do happen." It was the first time I had ever seen a trucker getting a speeding ticket.

It's not that I am hostile toward big trucks. But I must confess it is gratifying to know that occasionally trucks are subject to the same speed laws as underling automobiles. How many times the vortex of trailing wind from a high-speed truck has almost sucked my car into its menacing dual wheels!

It is not my desire to be unkind to truckers in general. I am sure most of them are splendid, courteous and caring drivers. It's the few bullies and speed maniacs among them that I have difficulty appreciating.

I don't believe I am a vengeful person who enjoys seeing someone get a speeding ticket with a stiff fine. So to convince you that I'm not vindictive, I hope the driver of that stopped truck received only a warning ticket and a strong lecture on the dangers of speeding. But that's about as kind as I can be on his behalf for right now.

No squeeze, no lemonade.

Context: Psalms 91:11

Nectar of the squeeze

An orange yields its best nectar when under a squeeze. The harder the squeeze, the more the nectar. And the sweeter.

What's true with oranges is true with life. No person is without "nectar" to give. But not everyone gives it. The squeeze is too dreadful to bear. Or harsh. Or lasting. But again, no squeeze, no nectar.

How many people would you classify as truly "great"? Winston Churchill surely qualifies. Yet Churchill passed through the squeeze of his "Wilderness Years" before the nectar of his eloquence could rally and sustain his besieged island of people. Martin Luther King qualifies, too. But he suffered the terrible squeeze of bigotry and of being black before he could inspire and summon the white masses to his "mountain top." And above all, there is that unschooled country preacher from Nazareth. He endured the horrible squeeze of a criminal's cross. It was the most brutal squeeze of all. But the nectar that flowed out from that cross became vital nourishment for humanity's sin-sick soul.

Squeezes are always unpleasant. Sometimes they are painful. Yet those squeezes extract from us lasting benefits for others. And for God.

Curse not your squeeze, then. Nor run from its grip. For in a little while, the residue it leaves just may serve as nutrients for someone else's life.

Fresh day, fresh affection.

Context: Proverbs 31:12

Spouse squelch

Spouses are a wonderful invention. Most of the time. At other times, they drag up pertinent points with which to squelch our comeuppance.

Several years ago I preached a series of sermons on the "Fruits of the Spirit." Noble words like love, patience and gentleness walked themselves around our house for several weeks.

Sometime later, I was rearranging some of the books in my library. Inscribed on the flyleaf of one book was a notation from my wife, Lavell. The book was a special gift from her during my seminary days. Her words of affection were especially meaningful and precious to me.

Later still, we were in the car driving to some meeting somewhere. Teasingly, I brought up the book and its inscription. Needling her a bit, I said, "I don't hear such affectionate words much anymore. What happened?"

I shouldn't have opened up the subject. With that series of sermons fresh in her mind, she replied, "Well, those words in the book were written before I discovered all the other *fruits of the spirit* in your life!"

I'll bet she had just been waiting to say that to me.

There are other books in my library inscribed with her bygone words of affection. But I've decided not to hunt any of them up. Instead, I'll be working on developing new skills to merit fresh affections of her heart.

Indeed, spouses are a wonderful invention. Most of the time. I think.

Enough is no longer enough.

Context: 2 Timothy 4:3

Insatiable stimulation

We were in a large department store, viewing the banks of televisions being demonstrated. Soon, one of the clerks came over. He began to explain how the video cassette players worked.

One model was so sophisticated that it could divide up the screen with one part showing the videotape and the other part showing regular programming. I wondered how on earth I could ever concentrate on two television pictures at one time.

The clerk must have noticed my deficient mentality. Right away he gloated, "In a few months we'll be coming out with a unit that can divide the screen into nine simultaneous programs. Then you will be able to view all the sports events at one time."

Good Grief!! Not only is that too much for two eyes

to focus on and two ears to cope with, but it's just too much for the brain to coordinate. Yet I suppose there will be countless bleary eyes, deaf ears and baffled brains by late fall—all trying to sort out if a touchdown was a homerun or a hole-in-one on a soap opera.

I had to get out of there before the future frightened me to death in the present. "One picture" is no longer adequate. "Two pictures" are fast becoming old hat. Only "nine pictures" will now do. But for how long, I wonder.

Such notions are just more evidence of our ravening appetite for the exotic and bizarre. The end result can be only spent reason and new regret.

The light we follow
is the end we find.
Context: Proverbs 16:25

Taillights

Finding himself in endless dense fog, a driver became panicky. The road was winding, so he quickly lost direction. Suddenly, taillights popped up ahead of him. Relieved, the driver said to himself, "At least I can see them. I'll just follow the taillights."

Closely he tagged along. Without warning, the taillights came to an abrupt halt. The driver crashed into the car ahead. Disgusted, the man rolled down the window and yelled into the fog, "For heaven's sake man, why didn't you signal that you were stopping?"

Back came the annoyed reply, "Why should I? I'm in my own driveway!"

Life is ever a journey. Frequently, we find ourselves in the thick haze of ambiguity. It is difficult to discover the clear truth. Or how far we are from it. We strain to see what is up ahead, where the curves are and where the drop-offs are waiting.

We hear voices of life clamoring for our attention and loyalty. But we can't discern from what direction they come. Nor how near they are. Nor even to where they lead.

Thus we grab hold of any distinguishable light that seems to be moving ahead. We fall in line behind whatever fad or fashion looks promising at the moment.

But following blindly behind whatever "taillight" pops up in the thick haze of ambiguity often leads to surprising and unfortunate ends. We are apt to find life crashing into shambles on an alien driveway of someone else's destination.

"I am the way!" Jesus said. That's the one beacon safe in all circumstances to follow—but especially so when we find ourselves in the fog of confusion.

What next is the real issue.

Context: 2 Kings 23:35

Taxes, death and what next

All day long a good man slumped over the dining room table, working on tax forms. By late afternoon he was fast approaching incivility. Coffee cup stains on the tablecloth matched his mottled disposition.

"There's one thing about life and taxes," he growled. "When you are finished with the former, you are through with the latter."

Trying to cool down the gathering steam storm, his wife replied, "It's not necessarily so, dear. It all depends upon where you wind up."

If you are heaven-bound when death takes you, you are indeed "through with taxes." Only perpetual dividends await you. But if you are headed toward the other destination when death comes, watch out! There's an awful "after-death tax" yet to be paid. Not only is that tax heavy, its burden lasts forever.

Filing tax reports seems to include a tendency toward self-destruction. Pray, then, that death doesn't greet you while you are slumped over your tax forms. Some people have been suspected of nullifying a lifetime of morality while toiling over their tax statements.

Can you imagine it? Here's neighbor John who, because of a single tax report, arrives at that other place. And promptly he is handed a bill that reads: "After-Death Taxes Due Forever."

Taxes, death and what next? These are vital issues for consideration while we are yet alive. And, as is so often the case, the last one is most important. For if daily we tend to the "what next," we likely will avoid any "taxes due" after the certainty of death.

Struggles make strongest disciples.

Context: 2 Corinthians 3:2-3

Trying times

Trying times! Tough sledding! Dark days! Call them what we will, we all know them. We know, too, that "trying times" are the wrong times to quit trying.

Most of the worthwhile achievements we leave as our legacy are those that struggled their way upward by way of hard times. That's why "hard times" are merely the precursors of "good times." Hard times give flavor to the flow of life.

I have known moments of exasperation from not being able to seize immediately the words I needed to express what I wanted to write. And for a preacher, not to be able readily to grasp adequate words with which to wrap and ship his ideas is misery equal at least to heartburn—especially when the deadline is already arriving at his doorstep.

Many times I have spun away from my desk and stalked out of the study, mumbling to an invisible audience, "The words are just not there! I quit!"

In the past, I know my family must have heard me coming and said to each other, "Watch it! Here comes Dad! Don't cross him, lest he explode with words readily available but inappropriate!"

Again and again I've returned to that still spinning chair. Trying moments or not, I had to keep at it. And invariably the right words would march themselves out to take their proper places.

Welcome your "trying times," then. Embrace them! For out of them are apt to come a much finer edition of what you are trying to write with your life.

Today, all things are new.
Context: Philippians 3:12-14

Using up today

"Never let yesterday use up today." Wisdom is remembered longest when wrapped in brevity.

Regularly we need to pause and assess just how much of today is used up with yesterday. Carryover disappointments have a way of embezzling today. Hangover anger is good at consuming the value of a new day. Even basking in the thrill of some past achievement subtly siphons off the opportunities of the present.

Several years ago I got to know an interesting but rather strange man. He was a delightful storyteller. For hours he could spin fascinating yarns that held the listener spellbound.

But as I reflect on that man's abilities, I realize his spellbinding tales were always woven from the fabric of yesterday. Much of his present served as the fodder of his past.

The only time we have to live is this present, passing hour. If we would make this fleeting hour count, therefore, we will employ it fully today. Otherwise, we are subject to double jeopardy. One, we are bound to live life every day on the same boring terrain where we've already traversed. Two, we are bound to expend double energy on concerns that keep coming around.

Living on the old terrain is not much fun. Expending double energy is not very productive.

When you exit today, close quickly the door behind you. Lest yesterday creep out to overtax today.

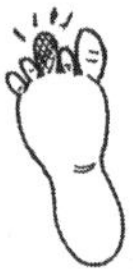

Pain often reminds of blessings.

Context: Luke 6:25

Parable of the middle toe

Life lessons come at odd times and in strange places. Recently, I learned the middle toe is far more sensitive to pain than the big toe. I know what I'm talking about. If you doubt me, take a small hammer, bang your big toe and your middle toe, and then see which one overrides the other in pain.

Barefooted, I made my way hurriedly to the closet to select shoes for the day. Nearing the closet, I rammed my middle toe into the partially opened closet door. Strange gyrations ensued as I hopped about on my left leg, cradling my right foot in my hand. I talked gently to my toe. I even spoke a word or two to God about it. Never in all my years has an injured big toe given me so much searing pain.

When a middle toe is mortally wounded, nothing seems to help—not even the temptation to dismantle a closet door. Nor the well-intentioned words of a loved one. All I wanted to do was blow on my toe, rub it gently and cry.

Plopping down on the end of the bed, I caressed my toe and promised it I would be more careful if it would forgive me and quit hurting.

Tears dried as I thought how ridiculous I must have looked and sounded. I also thought how fortunate I was to own eight pairs of shoes. How fortunate indeed, when most people in the world have no shoes at all. Their toes are subject constantly to all kinds of bumps, barks and bangs.

Suddenly the pain in my toe was transferred to my soul. And I could no longer feel sorry for myself.

Greeting tomorrow from afar.

Context: 2 Timothy 2:21

Greeting tomorrow from afar

Somewhere I read of a motel owner in a small town. An overnight guest stood at the checkout counter. "How's your motel business doing?" the guest asked cheerfully.

Without looking up from figuring the man's bill, the owner said somberly, "Well, I've never made enough money to stick it out. But I've never lost enough to get out. I'm just hoping to do one or the other this year."

That's the way it is with many of us. The economy of our faith is just active enough to keep us in the ranks of the religious. But not so little as to help us get out altogether. So we just wait to see what tomorrow will help us to do.

It's true that none of us knows what tomorrow might bring. But all of us can determine what we bring to it. Bankruptcy on the edge of tomorrow might take us down. A fire or storm might snatch our "motel" from us. We may even fall victim to some dread disease.

Any or all of these are possibilities. We never know. But in the meantime, we can greet tomorrow from afar. We can determine what we shall bring to the oncoming unknown. That way, our past will always serve to undergird us. And our present will seldom overwhelm us.

But just waiting to see what tomorrow brings us is to be ever looking downward, figuring up the bill for whatever business is at hand—only to look up to greet all the options already made for us.

Air travel, is it! Or?
Context: Job 39:27

Air travel

Air travel has been making news for years. Little of that news is encouraging. Revenge rationale blows up planes in mid-air. Aging aircraft give up doors and tops in mid-flight. Wages and working conditions pit employees against management. Bankruptcies and layoffs are familiar jargon of the industry.

I don't entirely enjoy flying. Its chief advantage is speed. Those things I dislike are many. Nearly 50 percent of the flights I've booked this past year were delayed several hours or canceled altogether.

Then there are those lines you stand in. Every several minutes you get to "foot-scoot" your baggage toward the counter as the incessant click of a computer facilitates another weary passenger. Next is that mob that rushes forth to crumple dignity at the gate.

Then there is that voice telling you how lucky you are to be on the latest "wide body" plane, which is just as snug as any earlier editions. And, of course, there are those quick-print, prepackaged meals that are almost enjoyable, except for a visiting elbow from the seat on either side.

But two "blessings" are really notable, especially on long flights. One is all the legroom you are rationed. Kneecaps get dents in them. The neck gets a crick or two. Both become souvenirs of the flight.

The other is being seated by some two-legged specimen of an obese hangover, who acts like the only way to get over it is to keep drowning it.

If I sound a bit critical, I'd say I was about typical. Maybe we weren't meant to fly after all. And that these "amenities" I've mentioned are God's way of reminding us.

Not true: Treasure today, trash tomorrow.

Context: 2 Timothy 2:21

Treasure

While engaged in one of my unannounced desk-cleaning-out forays recently, I came across a pen I had deposited into a drawer several years ago. I had "laid it to rest" for the time being. For two decades it had served as my favorite writing instrument. It had been the confidant of many of my most private thoughts. It had written me through countless pages of sermons, letters and manuscripts. For a moment I just stared at that pen, turning it tenderly in my hands. It was worn out, useless by most standards. "Time to throw it away," I thought. But I just couldn't do it.

I simply could not evict such an intimate and faithful friend. We had been through a lot together. Many times it had formulated some of my most intense frustrations. It had been party to my innermost thoughts—

good and bad. Obediently, it had scrawled cutting letters of anger and malice, knowing what it wrote would never be mailed. That pen had been through so much with me, I just couldn't toss it away in callous disregard.

Suddenly that scratched up and scarred pen took on special value. It became a real treasure to me. I realized afresh that "real treasures" always last longer than the time it takes to wear them out. I realized also that real treasures are never subject to rusting. Or rotting. Or running out of value.

So while cleaning out a clogged-up desk drawer, I discovered a new kind of treasure. They are the "pens" with which we write out the saga of God's dream for us.

Always there's reason to be grateful.

Context: Psalms 46:1

Trouble double

Flash floods drowned all his livestock. Standing water rotted the crops in the fields. Raging currents swept his house into the next county. The week before, the doctor had said the man had both ulcers and gout. The day before the flood, his only daughter ran off to join the carnival with a man twice her age. Clinging to each other atop a hill, the man and his wife overlooked the shambles of their lives.

Later, at a Chinese restaurant, friends and neighbors offered words of concern and encouragement to the couple. Suddenly, the restaurant rocked as the man shouted, "Well thanks be to God."

Embarrassed, his wife said, "Be quiet! We've got problems enough without your foolishness."

Handing her the "fortune" from inside his fortune cookie, the man said, "Read that!"

Her eyes twinkled as she read the fortune: "Serious trouble will pass you by!"

Shouting herself, the wife yelled, "Well, thanks be to God, indeed! The *serious stuff* is going to miss us!"

The whole restaurant joined in laughter. Life was getting better already.

No matter what calamity happens to us, there is always "serious trouble" that could be much worse. Catching the itch is bad trouble. Having no means to scratch it is "serious trouble." Falling out of a window is a terrible crisis. Stopping suddenly is the "serious stuff."

We are seldom in such a fix that we are beyond even worse circumstances. To keep that in mind makes coping with trouble more productive. And perhaps a bit gratifying.

Truth is heavier than weight.
Context: John 8:32

Scale truth

What a wonderful Father's Day gift I received! A new bathroom scale. The old one was unpredictable.

"We've got to get a new scale," I'd muttered regularly over the last year or so. "Old Faithful changes its integrity by several pounds over a single day." Trying to stabilize my weight was like trying to steady Jell-O.

So the new scale was welcome. Until, that is, I stepped aboard. Four pounds above my "actual" weight! Already!

"It's out of adjustment," I said. "There, it's on zero."

I stepped on again. Same story.

"It's the carpet," I rationalized. Placing it on a tiled area, I stepped up again.

"Like it or not!" the dial seemed to yell, "four pounds overweight!"

"Well, drat!" I muttered to myself. "This one's a fibber like the old one."

Quickly a scheme blossomed.

"I'll exchange it for an honest specimen."

By then I was chuckling inside.

What we won't do to make the bottom line tell us what we want to hear. We'll beg, barter or buy to hear it. If the instructions are not what we like, we hurry off to change the instrument. If the Lord God won't say to us what we want to hear from Him, we'll just trade Him for some homemade model that will. All of that is just a ploy to dodge and devalue the truth about us.

Facing truth is usually uncomfortable. But most of us know it is a healthy and necessary experience. For it is still the truth that sets us free.

So I've decided to keep the scale and to trust its truth. That way I'll be free to bring my weight into line with its honesty.

Truth hurts only to help.
Context: Zechariah 8:16

The truth hurts

Two high-strung brothers, who kept their household on the edges of incivility, came crashing out of the back door into the yard. All sorts of beast-like shrieks erupted from their vocal cords, to say nothing of their subhuman antics. It was enough to send neighbors scurrying for storm cellars.

The mother of the pair was chatting with a neighbor across the backyard fence. Seeing the horror in the neighbor's face, the mother said pleadingly, "Please don't let those boys get to you, too. They've already driven me batty." Then, pausing pensively, she said, "I really don't know which I'd rather they do—go around telling lies about our home life or go around telling the truth."

The truth hurts. Don't let anyone tell you it doesn't. It hurts sometimes even more than a lie. It hurts in many places, too, like the bathroom scale.

Of course, we can tamper with the scales to make them read whatever it takes to make us feel good. But truth will hurt a moment later when we walk to the closet and find our clothes have somehow shrunk.

Truth hurts, too, when a "white lie" (which is but a dark specimen bleached by our rationalizing) comes home to roost. Pietro Aretino said, "I'd rather you hate me for telling the truth than to adore me for telling you lies." That's a pretty heavy "druther." But it is the standard by which we live daily, if we would be disciples of truth ourselves.

What can aid us
often assails us.
Context: Proverbs 30:5

Unruly umbrellas

"If I miss heaven," I muttered to myself, "it will be due much to rebellious umbrellas." I had paid too much for it in the first place. It must have known how I felt, for it was disloyal from the day I bought it.

I had trusted it to protect me on the way to the barber shop. Once inside, the pesky thing wouldn't catch in the "closed" position—again! Those waiting for haircuts must have sensed my rising rage. Finally I just "wrapped" it closed with the snap strap.

Later as I opened it out on the street, it exploded with all kinds of gyrations. Only part of it opened; the rest was warped upward. It looked something like a squeeze-dried Australian bush hat. Half of my light-colored suit began to freckle from ricocheting raindrops. The other half just turned dark with soaked splotches. I hoped no one would meet me. Or greet me. It was no time to be civil.

Back at the office, I tried once more to close it. No luck. Coming in behind me was a friend. In her hand was a fancy fold-up model, which she appeared to be choking into submission.

"Myrtle," I asked, "would you like to receive a defiant umbrella?"

Pointedly she replied, "No, thank you, I don't need another cripple." She then told of her umbrella disaster.

Now it looks like two of us will miss heaven on

account of rebellious umbrellas. But Myrtle and I do have one slight consolation. Where our umbrellas are sending us, it won't be raining anyway!

Forgiveness is nobler than fairness.

Context: Luke 15:22-24

Unfair! Unfair!

"It's just not fair!" complained a middle-aged father. "Not when you have to pay $12 for a $2 haircut that used to cost $1 when you had hair."

He's right! Few things are fair in this world. Life isn't. Taxes aren't. The weather isn't.

Daylight-saving time doesn't play fair. It adds to one end what it takes away at the other. Where's the fairness in that?

Growing older isn't fair either. Reflexes slow. Eyesight dims. Energy wanes. Hair turns gray or loose or both.

Indeed, the world just isn't fair. But not only for haircuts. In everything from kites to cars, it costs about three times as much to get one-third the value that will last about half as long.

We can't do much about most of the unfairness of our world. But we can do a whole lot about how we conduct ourselves right in the middle of this unfair world. We can take an unfair slur and respond with a compliment. We can take an injustice hurled at us and rebound it as a blessing. We can even take the tragic diagnosis of "terminal" and redeem it by our prognosis of "righteous suffering."

No, it's not a fair world. Even God, in a sense, is unfair. If God were strictly fair, God would demand justice for our sinning rather than forgive us. In the things that really matter, then, it's not so bad to live in an unfair world. For it's the unfairness that gives us cause to live at our best.

When used, be useful.
Context: Isaiah 53:1-6

Used to be useful

"I always wind up being used. I always seem to accommodate someone else's agenda." The person who spoke those words to me many years ago was already waist-deep in despair. No wonder!

Being used pushes pain into our lives at several points. It betrays the trust we place in those who play false with us. It belittles our own intelligence for not realizing we were being taken. It forces us to forgo some of our prior objectives and to reorder others.

I was a "greenhorn" pastor at the time those words were spoken to me. I'm sure I didn't do a good job of responding. I think I know now what I would say if those words were said to me today.

I think I would say, "Your being *used* is indicative of your being a trusting, vulnerable person. You look for the good rather than the ugly qualities of a person. That's worth a whole lot in this day and age."

Jesus was used. He looked for the best in those He encountered. In doing so, He opened himself to their mean motives. They aimed to kill him, and they did. But the "used" Teacher from Galilee turned out to be their Savior. And ours.

The next time you feel used, don't wallow in despair. Or become bitter. Instead, thank God for the gift of a trusting heart.

That may seem a sign of weakness. But as you rise above being used, you become the instrument of your *user's* salvation. And that's the sign of real strength indeed.

Climbing and building:
the rhythm of life.

Context: Isaiah 40:4

Valleys

"How do I get out of this awful valley, where sheer cliffs hem me in on all sides, and I'm so utterly alone?" It's one of those *silent* questions rumbling around in the souls of lots of people. It's one of those questions many of us feel but want to keep quiet.

Eventually everyone becomes victim of a valley. Who hasn't found himself swallowed up in the valley of faded hope? Who of us hasn't fallen into the gripping valley of grief? Who among us hasn't felt "utterly" alone in some secret suffering? Not many of us could raise our hands to say, "I haven't."

When boxed in by sheer cliffs, two escapes are open. One is to climb out. That means to don climbing gear and start scaling the cliff's face. The top is attainable, if the gear and faith fail not. Or we don't fall.

That is the shortest way. But it is to trust our own strength and to work against gravity's pull.

The other way is to build our way out by deeds of love extended to others. We build upward when we befriend someone abandoned and alone in his valley. We build our way out by taking another's pain into our own heart.

Climb out or build out? Both are honorable. Climbing gets you out faster, but it is more arduous. Building gets you out slower, but it has triple advantage. One, it gets your mind off your own valley. Two, it serves as "fill dirt" that lifts to the top. Three, it usually brings someone else along.

I have a feeling, then, that the last is the most honorable way.

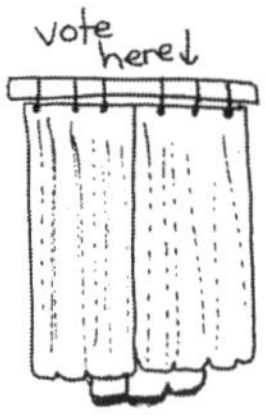

Dead or alive–we vote.

Context: 2 Corinthians 3:2-3

Your vote!

Someone told of a little old lady from downstate Illinois who had been a staunch political party member. Nearing death, she made one last request to her bedside relatives.

"When I pass on," she wheezed, "I want to be buried in Chicago."

Startled, her favorite nephew asked, "Auntie, why would you want to be buried in Chicago?"

Mischievously the woman gasped, "So I can go on voting."

We are both amused and outraged when "funny votes" are reported in public elections. In some elections dead people have cast some votes. It isn't entirely absurd, therefore, to conclude some people have actually served terms of office by vote of the dead.

It's a fascinating notion—this being able to vote after you are laid out to rest. Yet there is more substance than fiction to the idea.

How many of us find the lingering values of our parents still shaping our behavior? Which one of us hasn't—in the grip of temptation—heard in our soul the whispered counsel of a friend or mentor? Indeed, the dead are still casting their votes!

Among the crucial concerns in our here and now, then, just has to be what kind of votes we are casting today. For what we say, do and become, even right now, keeps on voting in the hearts and souls of those we leave behind. Dead or alive, we vote!

The middle is not always the most.

Context: Matthew 4:18-22

Wallowing in the middle

I keep a small book of cartoons on my desk. Some friends gave it to me. When things get muddled or bogged down, I flip through it for a little distraction. One cartoon turned me around recently.

Several people were gathered in a classroom. Apparently the instructor had called for comments. One well-dressed participant was standing and saying, "But I don't want to be *first*. Or *last*. I just want to wallow somewhere in the middle."

Among the well-dressed masses of the "middle"—that's where lots of us feel most comfortable. Somewhere in the middle, where it is cozy. In the middle where mediocrity mingles well with midget-mindedness and the short view of things.

But even a cursory glance at history tells us that milestones of human advancement have never come from the ranks of the middle. Milestones, for the most part, have risen out of laboratories of loneliness from people on the cutting edges of tomorrow.

A lowly Galilean routed his life around the ranks of the regulars. He called unto himself 12 ordinary artisans. He planted a dream in their souls. He said to them, "You might be more at home wallowing out your lives in the mediocrity of the middle. You might even feel safer. But if you would find life, risk it with me!"

They took up the challenge. They walked away with him. And without realizing it, they walked themselves indelibly into the ranks of human greatness. The invitation still stands. So does the opportunity.

Questions ask for answers. Answers interpret questions.

Context: 1 Peter 4:8

Say what?

Coming to a bus-stop bench, a weary tourist in New York City sat down for a brief rest. At the other end was a tarnished hippie who was swaying to the music coming over an earphone. Since the hippie seemed so much at home, the tourist asked, "Say, fellow, how do I get to Carnegie Hall?"

Still swaying and snapping his fingers, the hippie

replied, "Practice man, practice!"

Isn't it interesting how there can be several legitimate answers to the same question. It's all a matter of whose ears are hearing what.

To a visitor wanting to tour Carnegie Hall, the question is simple: "How do I get to its location?" But the ear of a budding performer may well hear the question on a different wavelength. The performer's answer then may justifiably be "You get there by practice, lots of practice!"

If it is safe to assume many questions have more than one answer, then we have cause for temperance. We also have helped to explain the reason for political parties and religious denominations. Both are widely known for their "one-answer" postures.

Which then of the two is nearer the ultimate answer—tourists or hippies?

Who knows? Until the "one and only" ultimate answer is determined, perhaps the hippie holds the edge. But only if his answer—"practice man, practice"—pertains to the fine art of tolerance and acceptance.

Wings are for soaring.

Context: Psalms 55:6

Wings

I am told there is a species of ants that is born with wings to fly. Early on, however, they tear off their wings. Once torn away, the wings can never regenerate. Consequently, the ants inflict upon themselves an earthbound existence. They consign themselves to a ground-level future.

People sometimes do that to themselves. They tear off their wings. And from there, they never rise above levels of the common. What a shame!

Here is a brilliant scientist with the mind of a genius. In a laboratory his mental assets might well have discovered the cure for some dreaded disease. But he tore off his wings and traded them for a bottle. In time, the bottle became his miserable prison.

Again, here is a man of marvelous speech and eloquence. He might well have been a great orator of truth and honesty. But he tore off his wings, too, and became a standup comic of vulgar proportion. He relished in making people chuckle at smutty jokes when he could have moved their hearts and habits toward decency.

Here is a lovely woman in her early 20s with magnetic talent to teach children. They flock to her to hear another "magic" story. She turns out to be a "model" for a ragged magazine that exploits her beauty and turns it ugly. She tore off her wings to wallow on the garbage heap of spent passions.

People don't have to end up like wingless ants. Severed wings can grow again. The means is called forgiveness.

If we would be wingless, we can have it. If we would be re-winged, we can have that, too.

"Can be" often is more valuable than "what is."

Context: John 1:42

Watermelon wisdom

Somewhere I came across the story of a 10-year-old girl who stopped at a farmer's fruit stand. Nearby was a watermelon patch. She picked out a hefty melon.

"That one's $3," said the farmer.

The girl replied, "I've got only 30 cents."

Deciding to have some fun at the girl's expense, the farmer pointed to a small, immature melon still in the field. "How about this one for 30 cents?" he asked.

Quick as a flash the girl replied, "OK, I'll take it. But leave it on the vine. I'll be back for it in three weeks."

I can just see that farmer lifting his straw hat, scratching his head and wondering how so quickly he got taken by a 10-year-old. Two very valuable lessons rise out of that story. One for the "farmer" and one for the "girl."

The lesson for the farmer is this: Watch out! Never underestimate the savvy of a 10-year-old. Or anyone else, for that matter. Those we think know little about the complexities of life are so capable of cutting through them to redden our faces—leaving us scratching our heads and wondering how we got so easily taken for a dunce.

The lesson for the girl is this: Life often offers us budding opportunities at a reduced price. At the time they may look "green" and unpromising. But if we would believe in them enough to buy into them, they just might hand us tenfold value "three weeks later."

Jesus proved it. He picked out Simon when Simon was quite "green" and unpromising. But in just three years, Simon became the "Rock" upon which the church was founded.

Watermelon wisdom is still surprisingly valuable.

Words are never just words.

Context: Matthew 5:37

Value of words

When a high school test called for the motto on all our money, less than half the class answered correctly. "I've seen it a thousand times," one student said apologetically, "but all I could think of was 'God Bless America.'"

How is it that great themes for life become so commonplace we tend to ignore their value? "In God we trust" is a noble thought that accompanies most of us most everywhere we go. We tote it around in our pockets and purses. We exchange it for everything from candy to cars. It is the daily topic of many conversations.

About the only places we don't take it are to the shower and to bed. Yet I've heard that some sleep with it under the pillow. Apparently, "In God we trust" is not quite adequate security.

"I love you" is another one of those priceless phrases that carries precious freight. Yet those words, too, are employed with such low calorie casualness that they mean barely more than a "Ta-

Ta" between departing friends.

"Sticks and stones may break my bones, but words can never hurt me," says the children's rhyme. It's not true. Words are powerful. They can indeed hurt. They can also heal. They can even restore hope.

Words like "In God we trust" and "I love you" are words whose veins course with nobility and inspiration. They are words worth carrying around in our pockets and purses and holding dear in our hearts. They are words valuable enough to spend sparsely.

Why? Because words are never just words.

Up or down? Not either, but both.
Context: Philippians 4:11

For better or worse

It's always the season for resolutions, admonitions and sage sayings. At the risk of overloading the air, I would offer an insight or two.

If things are going just great for you right now, don't worry! They will get worse! By the same token, if things are really bad for you right now, be patient. They will get better. The sheer rhythm of life guarantees it.

Life is akin to a roller coaster. It zips along at flank speed, shoving us full face into the future. Without warning, it drops us brutally into some deep valley, pulling our hearts into our throats along the way and pushing our blood to our dizzying heads. The slump has come. Things are bad. At the bottom is little prospect except the steep hill ahead.

Then abruptly we feel the strong hand of gravity

restraining our ascent. In time we are at the top again, careening and swaying and drinking in the fast pace of the good life again. Things are just great. But don't worry. They will get worse.

About the time we learn things are always getting better or worse, we have lived up most of life. But right there we make one more great discovery. We find that life is lived most victoriously when—in its zips downward—we are but making ready for the upward climb ahead.

Such a discovery will not lessen the heaviness and dreariness we feel at the bottom. Nor will it lengthen our stay at the top. It will put purpose into both. It will also keep us from breaking faith with God and from inviting ourselves inwardly to be whimpering failures.

What isn't there, isn't.

Context: 1 Chronicles 28:9

Fluky flakes

Blizzards will make you see things for days that aren't there. While in the Oklahoma Panhandle, my wife, Lavell, and I endured a blizzard. We've been weather-skittish ever since.

The following week, Lavell returned our granddaughter to her parents some 200 miles away. I spent the morning working on a sermon. The forecast said cold temperatures, high winds and possible snow.

Suddenly the wind gusted. I jumped to the window to see overcast clouds. Flakes flew by my window on the gusts. Still skittish, I phoned Lavell at our son's home. "It's snowing here," I said. "Better come home before the blizzard hits." She left immediately.

Later, I ventured outside to check on the gathering snowstorm. It was strangely warm. And no snow.

"What's happened to the snow?" I muttered. Just then several pinkish blossoms from our ornamental apple tree zipped passed me on the gusting wind. "Uh oh!" I said. "That wasn't snow I saw through the window; it was blossoms." I felt plumb foolish.

Four hours later, Lavell came through the garage door. It was the first time in our marriage that I was reluctant to welcome her home.

"Where's all the snow?" she demanded. I just knew she would ask that. It was time I owned up to my blizzard-crazed mind. She wasn't much impressed, especially since she had driven like mad to beat the storm.

I was willing to keep all this confidential. But not Lavell. She shared my "pinkish snow" with a couple of blabbermouths.

I had to get the facts out to keep the truth from getting any more strained.

Clinging stupidity–our frequent apparel.

Context: Ecclesiastes 10:6

Of keys, doughnuts, sermon points

Walking down the office corridor, I tried not to stir up any attention.

"Hey, bishop," a colleague said, "someone's breaking into your car!"

Well, the word was out.

"No, he's not," I replied, "at least not illegally. He's our custodian trying to rescue my keys I locked in my car."

The reason I locked up my keys is explainable. On my way to the office, my mind began to distill an idea for a sermon. Since I was driving, I couldn't write it down. So I rehearsed it in my mind until I could stop the car.

Arriving at my parking spot, I turned off the ignition, laid the keys on the seat, fumbled for my calling card and scribbled down the point.

"There," I thought, "now the point is on paper."

I got out of the car, touched the automatic door lock and pushed the door shut.

As it was closing, I saw the keys on the seat. Why is it door handles and door edges become ungrabable once a car door starts closing?

Instinctively, I glanced around to see if anyone had seen me. There's nothing like trying to look composed and dignified when clinging stupidity is dripping off you on all fronts.

While the custodian labored, I went into the building to greet our volunteer workers.

"Have a doughnut," someone said graciously. I figured that would help my wounded disposition, as I left to get a cup of coffee to go with it. When I returned, the doughnut was missing. Someone else had already confiscated it.

Locked-up keys and missing doughnuts—the day

was getting off to a splendid start. All downhill.

Well at least the sermon point I wrote down was rescued. And employed. And worked. I hope.

Index by topic

Index by topic

Index by topic

Index by Biblical text

OLD TESTAMENT

Index by Biblical text

OLD TESTAMENT

Index by Biblical text

NEW TESTAMENT

Index by Biblical text

NEW TESTAMENT